THE GOD WHO ANSWERS PRAYER

THE WORK OF THE
FATHER, SON, AND SPIRIT IN PRAYER

David Clarkson

The God Who Answers Prayer:
The Work of the Father, Son, and Spirit in Prayer

Is a revised, abridged edition of

Faith in Prayer

By David Clarkson (1622-1686)

Published by

CORNER PILLAR PRESS
Forest, VA

Printed in the United States of America

ISBN: 978-0-9976251-1-0

cornerpillarpress@gmail.com
www.cornerpillarpress.com

Cover Design:
Mary Bethany Adams

Cover Layout:
Jonathan Harris

Front Cover Picture:
Les Planteurs de Pommes de Terre
Jean-François Millet (1861)

PRAYER TRILOGY
by Corner Pillar Press

THE GOD WHO ANSWERS PRAYER: THE WORK OF THE FATHER, SON, AND SPIRIT IN PRAYER
David Clarkson

THE RETURN OF PRAYERS: SOWING SEEDS OF PRAYER AND WAITING ON GOD FOR A HARVEST OF ANSWERS
Thomas Goodwin

IMPORTUNITY: REFUSING TO GIVE UP IN PRAYER
Christopher Love

Other Works from CORNER PILLAR PRESS:

The Fountain of Life: A Display of Christ in His Essential and Mediatorial Glory, John Flavel
Preparation for Suffering, John Flavel

"Completer to a Contender for the Faith" Series:

A Basket of Summer Fruit, Susannah Spurgeon
Edited and annotated by Jennifer Adams
In Love with Christ: The Narrative of Sarah Edwards,
Edited and annotated by Jennifer Adams
Ann Judson: Missionary Wife, VOLUME I of
The Lives of the Three Mrs. Judsons, by Arabella Stuart,
Revised, edited, and annotated by Jennifer Adams
Delighting in Her Heavenly Bridegroom:
The Memoirs of Harriet Newell, Teenage Missionary Wife,
Edited and annotated by Jennifer Adams
Following Her Beloved: The Memoirs of Henrietta Shuck,
Missionary Wife and Mother,
Compiled by Jeremiah Bell Jeter,
Edited and annotated by Jennifer Adams
With Cords of Love: The Memoirs of Elizabeth Dwight:
Missionary Wife and Mother,
Compiled by Harrison Dwight,
Edited and annotated by Jennifer Adams

Contents

Chapter 1

God's Promise to Answer Prayer

This is the confidence we have in him, that if we ask anything according to his will, he hears us.
I John 5:14

LET me prescribe some directions to stir you up to prayer, the observance of which will establish the heart and encourage faith as you approach God.

1. Get an assurance of your interest in the covenant; namely, that Christ has loved you and washed you from your sins by his blood, that he has given you his Spirit, and that you are reconciled to him and in his favor. If you are sure that you are one of his favorites, you may be sure that you have his ear. As acceptance of persons goes before acceptance of service, so assurance of salvation is the ground of confidence in prayer. "These things have I written, that you may know that you have eternal life and that you may believe on the name of the Son of God. And this is the confidence that we have in him, that if we ask anything according to his will, he hears us. And if we know that he hears us, whatever we ask, we know that we have the petitions that we desired of him" (I John 5:13-15). First, if you have assurance that you have eternal life, then you have confidence that he hears you.[1] If you know that you have a right to eternal life by faith, then you may be sure that he will hear and grant your petitions. He will not hear in vain but will make sweet returns to the petitions he hears. "If you abide in me, and my words abide

[1] If you do not know whether you have eternal life, please read chapter 7, "A Definition of Saving Faith."

in you, you shall ask whatever you will, and it shall be done unto you" (Jn. 15:7). First, assure your union with Christ, and doubt not your audience with the Father. As union goes before audience, so assurance of a right standing with God by faith in Jesus Christ goes before assurance of answered prayer.

Faith in its infancy may put forth some weaker acts of recumbence and dependence upon God for an answer to prayer, but till it is grown up to assurance, it cannot be confident that God will hear or answer.

2. Consider that the Lord is engaged to hear prayer. If the Lord is engaged, strong engagements lie upon him to hear. Faith may conclude that he will hear, for he cannot be false to his pledge. He is bound by his titles and attributes to be the God who answers prayer!

(1.) *His titles.* "O you who hear prayer!" (Ps. 65:2). It is one of his titles of honor that he is a God who hears prayer, and this title is as truly ascribed to him as his mercy or his justice. He hears all prayer. "Therefore, to you shall all flesh come" (Ps. 65:2). He never rejects any prayer, no matter how weak or how unworthy the petitioner may be.[2] All flesh! Would he then (might faith say) reject mine? No! "He is rich to all who call upon him" (Rom. 10:12). "You are plenteous in mercy to all who call upon you" (Ps. 86:5). He is "a rewarder of those who diligently seek him" (Heb. 11:6). This must be believed as certainly as we believe that God is. As sure as God is the true God, so sure it is that none who seek him diligently will depart from him without a reward. He rewards all seekers, and if all, why not you? You may as well doubt that he is God if you doubt that he will reward your prayer. "If any man lack wisdom, let him ask of God who gives to all men liberally and upbraids not, and it shall be given him" (Jms. 1:5).

---

[2] This is under the assumption that the petitioner is a true believer. If you are not sure whether you are a true believer, please read chapter 7, "A Definition of Saving Faith."

(2.) *His attributes.* Considering God's power and goodness, faith may conclude that God is both willing and able to hear. These attributes of God are strong supports of faith, like Boaz and Jachin, the pillars of Solomon's temple. *Boaz,* "In him is strength," meaning he is able, and *Jachin,* "He will establish," meaning he is willing (II Chron. 3:17). When you pray, consider:

[1.] God is able to hear and give what you ask. It is gross atheism to doubt this—it is to question God's omnipotence. If God is able to do all things, then surely he can do what you ask in prayer. Omnipotence has no bounds, no *nil ultra* to it, no limit to this but his will. "Whatever the Lord pleased, that he did in heaven and earth" (Ps. 135:6). Consider he can do,

First, *Abundantly* (Eph. 3:20). He can do more than we ask. We can think more than we have reason or necessity to ask, but he can do more than we can think, abundantly more, exceedingly abundantly more! He has done more at the requests of his people than we can ask, and he can do more than he has done.

Secondly, *Easily.* He can do the greatest thing you ask more easily than you can do the least thing you think. That which all the united strength of men and angels, the whole creation cannot do, or not without great labor and travail, he can do as easily as you can move a finger or turn an eye. He can do that with a word, with a look, what all the creatures in heaven and earth cannot do with their whole strength (Matt. 8:3). If he can work a miracle with a word, how easily then can he do all that you ask! And if it is so easy for him to grant, why should faith doubt?

Thirdly, *Safely.* He can answer your requests without any loss or damage to himself, without any diminution of that infinite store that is in himself. Whenever he gives, he never has the less, for he bestows favors as the sun communicates light. The sun loses nothing by shining. The more it shines, the more illustrious it is. Likewise, the more God bestows, the more his glory shines. All that you can desire is not so much to God as a drop is to the whole ocean. The sea would lose something, though an inconsiderable loss, by the subtraction of one drop; but God, whatever he gives, loses nothing because what he bestows are things without him.

[2.] God is willing to answer. Faith seldom questions God's power; that which hinders faith is doubting his willingness. There is no reason to question this, for he is as willing as he is able. His goodness is infinite. Nay, he is as willing (if not more willing) to hear you as you are willing to pray. He is as willing to grant your petition as you are to have it; nay, more willing, which appears from:

First, *His secret will.* He was willing, resolved, and determined to hear you before you were willing to ask. He decreed it from eternity. In fact, he was willing before you even had a will or existed. Furthermore, he was not only willing before you asked, but he is the reason why you are willing. You must not think that your prayers move God to be willing. His will is the same forever, not subject to the least motion or alteration. Prayers are a sign rather than a cause that God is willing. He is not made willing because we pray, but because he is willing, he stirs up our hearts to pray. "Lord, you have heard the desire of the humble. You will prepare their hearts, you will cause your ear to hear" (Ps. 10:17). He first desires to do us good and then makes us desire it and pray for it that we may have the mercy in his own way—a clear evidence that he is more desirous to give than we are to receive because he makes us willing to ask.

Secondly, *His revealed will.* He that prescribes the only course whereby prayer may get an audience without fail commands us to follow that course. The Lord prescribed such a course that prayer can never return without the desired answer, but the best of men are more or less negligent in observing this prescript. Therefore, he is more willing that our prayers should be heard than we ourselves are desirous of an answer.

Chapter 2

Christ's Intercession

He is able to save to the uttermost those who draw near to God through him since He always lives to make intercession for them.
Hebrews 7:25

NOW, since the Lord is willing, and so very willing to hear, why should we not believe that he will hear? What strong encouragement we have to pray in faith! There is as much reason to believe that God will hear as there is to believe that you are willing to be heard. You may as well doubt that you are willing to be heard as to that doubt God is willing to hear.

A great encouragement to faith in prayer is Christ's intercession. "Seeing that we have a great high priest that is passed into the heavens, Jesus the Son of God, let us hold fast our profession" (Heb. 4:14). "Let us come boldly unto the throne of grace that we may obtain mercy" (Heb. 4:16). Because of Christ's exaltation, you have confidence to speak all your mind and heart in prayer with assurance of prevailing. "Having boldness to enter into the holy of holies by the blood of Jesus, let us draw near with a true heart in full assurance of faith" (Heb. 10:19, 22). Why? Because you have a high priest whose office is to intercede. In him, as such, we may have access with boldness and confidence (Eph. 3:12). This affords many things to embolden faith and make it confident in its access by prayer.

First, *Christ appears in heaven for us* (Heb. 9:24). He entered into heaven for this purpose, and for this end he sits at the right hand of the Majesty in the heavens (Heb. 8:1). How confidently might you present a petition if assured that the one who not only has the greatest power, but all power in the court where you prefer it, would appear for you! Christ has all power in heaven and earth. In that court where your petition is to be presented, he appears for you and can do whatever he will in the whole world. Can you doubt but that your petitions will prevail when Christ owns you and stands up on your behalf?

Secondly, *Christ presents us unto God.* He presents us as acquitted from guilt, adorned with his righteousness, united to himself, in so near a relation as if to reject us were to reject Him. He presents us as free from whatever might exasperate justice, provoke wrath, or render us in our prayers the least bit unacceptable (Zech. 3:4). No filthy garments, nothing in our persons, so presented, can prejudice our petitions. This was typified by the high priest carrying the names of all the tribes on his breast into the holy of holies. He presents us to his Father as the travail of his soul, as though he should say, "Behold, I and the children whom thou hast given me." He presents us as those who are as dear to him as his own spouse. He takes us, as it were, by the hand and leads us to his Father and our Father (Eph. 3:12). He presents us as those who are as near to him as the members of his own body. In reference to that intimate union, we are said to "sit with him in heavenly places" (Eph. 2:6). He presents us in such a lovely, endearing posture that we need not doubt our acceptance. He said, "The Father himself loves you because he has loved me" (Jn. 16:27). When we are thus presented, there is no reason to doubt that the Lord will hold forth the golden scepter.

Thirdly, *Christ offers our prayers.* This was the high priest's office (Heb. 5:1; 8:8) who served as a type of Christ. The Father receives our petitions from Christ's hand (Rev. 8:4). Christ takes us in one hand and our petitions in the other, and in this engaging posture, he delivers our prayers. Can you, therefore, fear that the Lord will reject a petition delivered by the hand of Christ?

Fourthly, *Christ sanctifies our prayers and separates from them whatever is offensive.* The Levitical priests, who were to bear the iniquity of the holy things, were a type of Christ (Exod. 28:36, 88). When the Lord looks upon Christ, he takes notice of nothing but holiness in the prayers presented by him. Christ is always ready to present them. "He ever lives" to make intercession. He intercedes for us as Paul for Onesimus: "I beseech you for my son. . . . And if there be anything blame-worthy, put that on my account" (Phile. 10,18,19). Christ stands up as our advocate to prevent the prejudice that sin might bring to our prayers (I John 2:1). He not only petitions but pleads. It is just and right that the Lord should not take notice of the sin in our prayers because he has made full satisfaction for every sin and failing. If anything should make faith doubt the success of prayer, it is our sinfulness, but Christ prevents that, for he has so fully made satisfaction for sin that the Lord cannot take notice of it so as to be angry with our prayers. It is through the virtue of Christ's intercession that our prayers are not dead works but free from that guilt which would make them deadly. For this end, he entered into the holy place with blood (Heb. 9:12), sprinkling unclean prayers that they might be sanctified and pure (Heb. 9:13, 14). When they are thus purged, they are services acceptable to God (I Peter 2:5). It is Christ's work to purge. "He shall sit as a refiner and purifier of silver, and he shall purify the sons of Levi" (Mal. 3:3-4). Now, is there any room for faith to doubt here? Will not the Lord accept that which is rendered acceptable by Christ? Can he be displeased with that which through Christ is pleasant to him? Will he reject a peace offering? Christ's intercession leaves no exception. Will he deny a prayer against which he has no exception? Faith must either be confident here or entertain blasphemous thoughts of God.

Fifthly, *Christ answers all accusations that can be framed against our prayers.* Indeed, he undertook to remove all just ground of accusation. If there be any accusation, it suggests an insufficiency of his atonement. Therefore, it personally concerns him to vindicate our prayers, since if any exceptions can be taken to our prayers for the utter rejecting of them, his own merit and satisfaction is equally liable. Hence, he confronts Satan with such indignation for accusing Joshua, saying, "The Lord rebuke thee, Satan" (Zech. 3:1, 2). Likewise, because of Christ's satisfaction on his behalf, Paul's confidence rose up into a triumph. "Who can lay a charge against God's elect?" (Rom. 8:33). If our prayers cannot be charged with anything to hinder the Lord from answering them, why should we doubt that he will answer them? Will the Lord hearken to Satan rather than to his own Son? Here is a great reason for confidence in answered prayer—we must either believe God will answer or entertain the most horrid thoughts about him.

Sixthly, *Christ mingles his own prayers and intercession with our requests.* He joins us, and, as it were, petitions that our prayers may be received. He adds the virtue of his own merits to our prayers, and this, as incense, does sweeten and make them acceptable, so that these, and all other services, are like those contributions of the saints which Paul mentions (Phil. 4:18), being an aroma of a sweet fragrance, like Noah's offering, from which the Lord smelled a sweet savor (Gen. 8:21). This was typified by the legal service. While the people under the law were praying without, the priest offered incense within (Luke 1:8-10). Answerably, while we are praying, Christ offers incense to sweeten our prayers and make them ascend as a delightful fragrance before God (Rev. 8:3, 4).

Seventhly, *That Christ not only presents us and our petitions unto the Father,* but does, as it were, present a petition himself to the Lord that he would answer our prayers, so that if the Lord were to deny us, he must deny Christ, too; and will Christ be denied? We are as sure to be heard as Christ himself is to be heard. The Father always hears him (John 11:42; 12:28). No more certain ground of confidence in the world than Christ's prayer for us.

It is true that the Scripture, in describing Christ's intercession, uses some expressions which must not be taken literally, for if so understood, according to the letter, they convey something inconsistent with Christ's glorious state and his equality with the Father. Yet, we have ground enough to say and believe that Christ prays for us, for Christ himself said it (John 17). He did pray, and he promises he will pray (John 14:16; 16:26). Moreover, the Father expects and requires it even after his exaltation (Ps. 2:8).

There are four acts of Christ which amount to as much as prayers for us, are more than equivalent thereto, and afford more encouragement to faith than if he should now pray for us after the manner of men. I do the more willingly insist on this particular, that Christ's praying for us and the promised success of our prayers are such a confirmation of faith, leaving no room for doubting.

(1.) Christ's requests on earth, which are properly and formally a prayer, are no less effectual than if they were now made in heaven, for he is always heard, then as well as now (John 11:42). This prayer is delivered to us (John 17). Wherein, observe for whom he prayed (ver. 20), not only for his disciples but for all who shall believe to the end of the age. And observe for what—for all things that we stand in need of while we are on earth, nay, to all eternity. It is so comprehensive as there is nothing we can desire of God that in one way or the other cannot be reduced to one of his petitions, so that whatever we now need was already granted to Christ when He prayed for us. Therefore, our petitions are as good as granted before they are presented, Christ having already gone before us in requesting from his Father all that we can desire for ourselves. Therefore, when we go to pray, faith may be encouraged to consider that Christ prayed for us and was heard as to those very particular requests which we are praying.

(2.) The cry of Christ's blood is metaphorically, yet really, a prayer. It is a pleading, speaking blood. "It speaks better things" (Heb. 12:24). It is as effectual to procure the bestowing of those things which are purchased by it as innocent blood is to procure vengeance for those that spill it. Christ's blood is an importunate, prevailing advocate, and it is never non-suited. Its plea is justice. It is just that the Lord should hear our prayers since this was one end for which the blood of Christ was shed. It is just that our request should be granted since his blood was the price of this privilege. The Lord should be unjust and undervalue the blood of his Son if he should not give that which he shed his blood to purchase. You must either believe upon this consideration or blaspheme. It is the blood of the covenant by which the blessings of the covenant were purchased and are confirmed (Heb. 10:29). Now that is one article of the covenant, namely, that whatever we ask in Christ's name shall be given. His blood cries for the performance of this, and justice itself hears it. It is but a righteous thing in reference to Christ (though pure mercy to us) that all our prayers should be heard.

(3.) The will of his divine nature is transcendently a prayer. I call it a prayer because his prayer on earth runs in the same tenor. "Father, I will" (John 17:21). It is the will of Christ, as he is God, that all our prayers should be heard, else he would not so often promise it. It is a prayer transcendently because though it differs from ours in form, yet it infinitely transcends ours in efficacy. His bare will, as he is the exalted God-Man, is more effectual for the comfortable returns of our petitions than if while on earth he should prostrate himself and with strong cries and tears importune the Father to answer us. For his divine will is all one with his Father's will; they differ not. Therefore, if the Father should deny Christ, he should deny himself. Here is encouragement indeed. We may as well imagine that he will deny Christ as to doubt that he will deny us.

(4.) The desires of his human nature. This is effectually a prayer; it has all that is essential to a prayer. The voice and outward posture are but externals. It is a mental though not a vocal prayer. It has as much of a prayer in it as any angel or soul can make (I Sam. 1:18). This was his desire on earth, and this is his desire in heaven, that all our prayers are answered. His affection for us was not impaired by his ascension but rather improved, and he that was heard in that which he feared will be heard in that which he desires. Now let faith put all these together, and it will be easy to read the necessity of an answer. Let it observe the premises, and it may well conclude the Lord will answer. If the Lord will hear his Son, if he will not deny himself, if he cannot be unrighteous, if he cannot be changeable, then he will hear us.

Chapter 3

The Spirit's Assistance

❧

The Spirit also helps our weakness, for we do not know how to pray as we should, but the Spirit Himself intercedes for us with groans too deep for words.
Romans 8:26

THE Spirit has an integral role in prayer. He is the Spirit of supplication (Zech. 12:10). It is his function to intercede for us, to pray in us, and to help us to pray. He writes our petitions on our hearts. He composes to us a matter, and we express it in prayer. That prayer which we are to believe will be accepted is the work of the Holy Spirit. It is his voice, motion, operation, and so it is his prayer. Therefore, when we pray, he is said to pray. Our groans are his groans, and our designs and intents in prayer are his meaning (Rom. 8:26, 27). He joins with us in prayer and supports us under infirmities with his own strength. The fact that prayer is the work of the Spirit appears in many particulars:

(1.) *The Spirit stirs us to pray.* He prepares and prompts, incites and inclines the heart to make requests. He removes that backwardness, averseness, and unwillingness that is in us so we can perform this spiritual service. "You will prepare their heart" (Ps. 10:17). He prepares the heart by his Spirit. He intercedes for us. He excites us, provoking us to pray. No man of his own accord can speak one syllable in prayer," says Calvin, "but that God, by the secret instinct of his Spirit, incites the heart to it. He puts the heart into a praying frame and sometimes excites us so powerfully as we cannot withhold from pouring out our souls before him." As it was with the prophet in another case, "His word was in my heart as a burning fire" (Jer. 20:9), so as to prayer, the workings of the Spirit are sometimes so powerful in the heart and so fill the soul that it cannot contain it but must vent itself and pour out its requests. Thus it was with David. "I was dumb with silence. I held my peace even from good, and my sorrow was stirred. My heart was hot within me. While I was musing, the fire burned; then I spoke with my tongue" (Ps. 39:2, 3). Those who have the spirit of prayer do find this by experience, especially when the Lord is about to show them some special favor or do some great thing for them, that he stirs them up to seek it in prayer. So that often, if they observe it, they may discover the return of their prayers in the temper and workings of their hearts to it. The Spirit's preparing the heart to pray signifies the Lord will cause his ear to hear.

(2.) *The Spirit teaches us what to pray.* This is plain in the apostle's expression (Rom. 8:26-27). We know not what is proper and expedient for us, what is seasonable, what is best, or when it will be so. We, of ourselves, would be ready to ask that which is impertinent, unseasonable, or hurtful to ourselves. We would have ease, liberty, plenty, deliverance out of troubles, and freedom from sufferings. We would have joy and assurance, yea, triumphs and raptures. We would have these or the like presently, and in full measure, at such a time or in such a degree as might be prejudicial to our souls; and so we would seek them if we were left to ourselves, if the Spirit did not better direct us and lead us to what is most necessary, proper, and spiritually advantageous. The Spirit helps us to pray according to the will of God for such things as are according to his will. Ambrose said, "That the soul may pray well, the Spirit goes before it and guides it into the right way, that we may not seek what is carnal nor things that are either too small or too great for us." A good physician knows what diet is most proper and when it will be most for the advantage of health. The opportuneness of meat sometimes restores the health, which, if it is taken unseasonably, endangers the patient. Therefore, because we know not what to pray for and how we ought to seek it, the Spirit intercedes for us by directing us what to ask.

(3.) *The Spirit helps his people express their desires in prayer.* Therefore, that manner of praying seems best which gives most liberty to the Spirit in its workings and leaves us under his influence and assistance, not only as to the inward but also as to the outward manner of prayer, letting the Spirit clothe his own matter in his own dress and taking words from him when he is pleased to afford them. I do not say that all the expressions used by God's people in prayer are from the Spirit, nor that he always helps them in their expressions. Whether they have them by the use of such means as he has appointed and concurs with, or whether they have them by immediate suggestion, either way they are from the assistance of the Spirit. The fact that he is ready to assist them in some way, even as to the words, seems signified by the apostle's expression (Rom. 8:26-27) which I have opened before and shall now further insist on. The Holy Spirit is frequently called an Advocate, meaning one called in for the assistance of a client, for an advocate is the comfort and encouragement of his client. He advises him, pleads for him, moves for him, draws up his petitions or motions, and dictates the form or words. Now the Holy Spirit is an advocate for his people with men and with God. By observing how he performs this office with men, we may deduct how he performs it with God. He acts as an advocate with men by telling believers what to say when they are brought before men's tribunals (Mat. 10:20, Mark 8:11, Luke 12:11, 12; 21:14, 15). Likewise, he acts as their advocate with God by dictating or suggesting to them what they shall say in prayer when they come to the throne of grace. The best interpreters that I meet with explain the expression *Veluti verba et suspiria nobis intus dictat* to mean that the Spirit inwardly dictates to us words and sighs. He assists us by his holy inspiration both with powerful and effectual words and sighs. He tells us, as it were, what we shall say.

(4.) *The Spirit stirs up affections in prayer suitable to the subject,* whether joy or sorrow, or love and delight, with earnest desires. He fills the heart with affections and motions which manifest themselves by sighs and groans that cannot otherwise be expressed, being so full of affectionate workings as they cannot find vent by words.

A pretender to the Spirit has more in his words than is in his heart, but one effectually assisted by the Spirit has more in his heart than he can express in words. The words of the former overreach, but the expressions of the latter fall short of what they feel within. The Spirit helps his people sense their spiritual state, and he makes them sensible of their spiritual wants, their inward distempers, and their soul-grievances. He makes them apprehensive of the importance, necessity, and excellence of what they are to ask for, and incites love, desire, and fervor to pray accordingly. Those affectionate workings in their hearts which are too big to be let out by words, being signified by sighs and groans that cannot otherwise be uttered, are a work of the Spirit.

(5.) *The Spirit acts graces in prayer.* He helps the weakness and infirmity of spiritual habits and principles, drawing them out into vigorous exercise. He helps the soul approach God with confidence yet reverence; with filial fear, yet an emboldened faith; with zeal and importunity, yet humble submission; with lively hope, yet self-denial. As it is the Spirit of supplication, so it is the Spirit of grace who not only works grace in the heart but sets the heart to work in prayer.

(6.) *The Spirit removes or helps the soul against distempers which are ready to seize on the soul in prayer* such as distractions, straightness of heart, indifference, formality, lukewarmness, hypocrisy, weariness, pride, and self-confidence. Since much of prayer is to be ascribed to the Spirit, and since he gives both matter and form, expression and affection, and motion to the act, teaching both when, what, and how we should pray, and assisting us in it, well may believers' prayers be counted the work of the Spirit. This consideration affords great encouragement to faith. If prayer were only our own work, we might fear it would be rejected, for all our righteousness is as filthy rags. But the work of the Spirit must be acceptable, yea, it is accepted. If only we ourselves spoke, the Lord might shut his ear and refuse to hear. But prayer is the voice of the Spirit. He speaks in us and by us (Mat. 10:20). The Lord will certainly listen to that voice. Prayer is the motion of the Spirit, and whatever motion he makes in the court of heaven can never be rejected. If we prayed of ourselves only, the Lord might refuse to send any comfortable returns, but since the Spirit intercedes for us, the Lord cannot deny him, else he should deny himself. The Spirit intercedes as effectually as Christ intercedes, though not in the same manner. Christ intercedes by office while the Spirit intercedes by operation. Christ appears in person for us, pleading our cause himself. The Spirit inspires and assists us to plead our own cause in his name. Not only through Christ but by the Spirit do we have access to the Father (Eph. 2:18). Will the Lord exclude those who have access to him by his Spirit? The Spirit "strengthens us with might in the inner man" (Eph. 3:16), and the strength of the Spirit will prevail, as with Jacob. Come armed with this strength, and you may come boldly to his throne to find grace and help in time of need (Heb. 10:15, 19).

Chapter 4

The Father's Willingness

How much more shall your Father who is in heaven give good things to them that ask him?
Matthew 7:11

CONSIDER your relation to God. He is your Father. Christ teaches us to begin with this. This is a strong support to faith, and Christ makes use of it to encourage us to pray. "Ask, and it shall be given you; seek, and you shall find; knock, and it shall be opened to you" (Mat. 7:7-8). There is the promise or argument whereby he would persuade us to believe the promise in praying (Mat. 7:9-11). The Lord is as ready to give to those who ask as the most indulgent father is ready to give to his most favored child, nay, more ready, much more ready. "How much more shall your Father who is in heaven give good things to them that ask him!" (ver. 11). He is much more ready to give the greatest favors than earthly parents are to give the least. That which is *good* in Matthew is the *Spirit* in Luke 11:18. And what greater gift than the Spirit? There are many things that may hinder earthly parents, such as poverty or covetousness, but there is nothing to hinder God. He has infinite treasures and a large heart. He can give whatever we ask. "The earth is the Lord's," and he is more willing than the fact that the heavens are more above earth.

God gets glory by hearing prayer. We not only glorify him by praying, as I showed before, but he glorifies himself by answering. The Lord gets by giving. He gets that which is of more account with him than what he gives. It is his interest to grant as much as it is ours to receive. If the Lord should reject our prayers, he would reject his own honor.

Consider the nature and dignity of prayer which affords divers arguments to confirm faith in God's willingness to hear.

(1.) Prayer is God's ordinance, instituted and enjoined for this end. He commands us to pray that we may be heard. Ordinarily, when you meet with a command, you find a promise. "Call upon me in the day of trouble, and I will answer" (Ps. 50:15). "Ask, and you shall have" (Mat. 8:7-8). When God commands prayer, he promises an audience. It was his intention in this institution. Therefore, if the Lord should not hear, his ordinance would be in vain, and the Lord should lose his end. Is it not easier to believe that the Lord will hear than to believe that he will come short of his end?

(2.) In Scripture, God adorns prayer with many transcendent privileges that fortify the most languishing faith. There is a strength in prayer which has power with God. "By his strength he had power with God; yea, he had power over the angel and prevailed. He wept and made supplication unto him" (Hos. 12:3-4). That strength was weeping and supplication. With this he wrestled (Gen. 32:24). He had power, *i.e.,* he was a prince with a princely deportment. Poor dust and ashes in a praying posture are in the state of princes, honorable and powerful princes, such as the Lord will not resist; therefore, prayer must prevail. The Lord may seem to wrestle as though he would give a refusal to prayer, but this is only to exercise the strength of this princely champion. He honors prayer so much as to always allow it to prevail. No wonder prayer is powerful, for it lays hold on God's strength. In this manner, some apply the verse from Isaiah, "Let him lay hold of my strength that he may make peace with me, and he shall make peace" (Is. 27:5). The Lord, for our encouragement, condescends to express the power of grace in such terms as though it laid some restraint upon his infinite being.

"Leave me alone" (Ex. 32:10). He is so unwilling to deny prayer that it is as though he is unable to act against it. This is a transcendent expression, "Thus says the Lord, the Holy One of Israel, and his Maker, 'Ask me of things to come concerning my sons; and concerning the work of my hands, *command me*' " (Is. 45:11). A wonderful indulgence, an astonishing condescension! As though asking were commanding. It is blasphemy to imagine that the creature should command the sovereign Majesty of heaven, yet we may safely infer that prayer shall surely prevail as though it could command God. Prayer shall prevail as much with God, though He is infinitely above us, as we can do with those who are under our command.

(3.) Prayer is the Lord's delight. It is the most pleasing service we can ordinarily tender. Therefore, he does not most frequently command it but importunately pleas with us to do it! "Let me hear thy voice," says Christ to his spouse, "for thy voice is sweet" (Cant. 2:14). It is a sweet incense (Ps. 141:2), being his delight (Prov. 15:8). It ascends as the fragrance of a sweet aroma; no sacrifice is more acceptable. One sincere prayer pleases God more than hundreds of rams or thousands of rivers of oil. Therefore, after he had declared how little he needs or regards sacrifices and burnt-offerings, he tells what would please him most. "Offer unto God thanksgiving, and pay your vows to the Most High, and call upon him in the day of trouble; I will deliver you, and you shall glorify me" (Ps. 50:14-15). The reason that he will answer your prayers is that it most glorifies him. It acknowledges and gives a clear testimony to his glorious perfections, power, wisdom, bounty, goodness, immensity, all-sufficiency, and providence. Now that which most glorifies him most pleases us, for his glory is the end of all his administrations. Now, will the Lord reject that which pleases him? Will he not listen to that wherein his soul delights? Will he not make gracious returns to that which is the most acceptable service?

(4.) He threatens men for not answering when others cry for help. "Whoever stops his ears to the cry of the poor, he shall cry himself but not be heard" (Prov. 21:18). Now, will he not do that himself for which he threatens us if we do not do (Mat. 18:28)? He will deal severely with those who will not hearken to the importunity of such as seek help in their want and distress.

The things prayed for afford arguments for faith. Either they are of great consequence or of small consequence. If small, then faith may argue, "Will the Lord stand with me for small things? Will he deny inferior mercies? Will he who has granted greater things deny less? Will not infinite love vouchsafe small favors? Will he who has given me Christ deny anything, any small thing? Will not he who has delivered your souls from death deliver your feet from falling?" If of great consequence, faith may argue, "Though it is great, yet the Lord has already granted greater to me. Is anything greater than Christ? Is anything of more importance than pardon of sin? Is anything more precious than the blood of Christ? I can ask nothing so great but the Lord has already granted greater." Or suppose it is the greatest thing that ever was granted to you or desired by you—well then, the greater it is, the more encouragement to ask it and the more hope God will grant it. It becomes the great God to grant great things, "To him alone who does great wonders" (Ps. 136:4). When you ask great things, you ask such as becomes God to give, "whose mercy is great above the heavens" (Ps. 57:10). Nothing under heaven can be too great for him to give. The greater things he bestows, the greater glory redounds to his name. Great and wondrous works speak the glorious honor of his majesty (Ps. 145:5). Great dignities show their magnificence by great presents. It is their delight and honor. God shows his infinite greatness by doing such things and bestowing such favors as are above the creature's power. Jehoshaphat argued, "Are you not God in heaven, and do you not rule over all the kingdoms of the heathens? And in your hand is there not power and might so that no one is able to withstand you?" (II Chron. 20:6). But suppose the greatness of what you desire does discourage, consider it is great only in your apprehension. Nothing is great to God. See how he is described (Is. 40:15, 17, 22). What is greater than this vast fabric of heaven and earth? How did the Lord make this only with a word? Let there be, and it was so (Ps. 33:6). This manner of expression tells us the effecting of the greatest things is no more to him than the speaking of a word is to us (II Chron. 14:11; I Sam. 14:6). It is all one with God to save by many or by few, to do that which seems great to us as that which seems small.

Consider the promises. The Lord has promised he will hear. If you doubt he will hear, you doubt he is faithful. Consider how many, how universal, how engaging are his promises.

(1.) The *Multitude.* There is no duty and no act to which the Lord has made so many promises as to prayer. Now, why should the Lord multiply his promises except that he will never fail to answer and that he would have us to be confident that we shall never fail in asking?

(2.) The *Universality.* He has promised again and again to hear whoever prays and to grant whatever is prayed for. Whoever prays, whatever they pray for, they shall be answered. It shall be granted. *Whoever:* "Whoever shall call on the name of the Lord shall be delivered" (Joel 2:32; Acts 2:21). He is "plenteous in mercy to all who call upon him" (Ps. 86:5). He is "near to all" (Ps. 145:16) and "rich unto all" (Rom. 10:12). *Whatever:* "All things you shall ask in prayer, believing, you shall receive" (Mat. 21:22). "Whatever you shall ask the Father in my name, he will give it you" (John 16:23). "Whatever we ask, we receive of him" (I John 3:22). "Ask what you will, and it shall be done unto you" (John 15:7).

(3.) The *Obligement.* The promise to answer prayer is more engaging to him than an oath. He values it more than we value our lives. It is more valuable to him than heaven and earth. He will suffer these to perish rather than a jot of his word to fail. "Heaven and earth shall pass away, but my word shall not pass away." The Lord would lose more by failing to answer your prayers than you would lose by failing to get an answer. His promise is engaged for your security, which is more precious to him than anything you ask. His word, truth, faithfulness, seal, oath, and the blood of his Son are all engaged in a promise to answer your prayers.

Consider the success of others, how effectual the prayers of God's ancient people have been; this affords great encouragement.

(1.) You never find any prayer wholly denied. In all the Scripture, not one example of a faithful prayer went without a gracious return. God never said to the house of Jacob, "Seek my face in vain." Those instances which seem to contradict this do confirm it. David prayed for the life of his child and prevailed not, but his prayer was answered in that the Lord gave him another child, honorably born and rarely endowed. Moses prayed that he might take possession of Canaan. While he was not heard as to that particular, the Lord gratified his prayer by showing him what he desired in a miraculous way. Moreover, he committed the conduct of the Israelites to his servant, Joshua, and instead of letting him enter the earthly Canaan, he translated him to the heavenly Canaan, where Moses could acknowledge that it was the sweetest return of prayer he had ever experienced. Though on earth he complained that the Lord would not hear him, yet there he praises the Lord for so answering his prayer. So, if the Lord never denied prayer, will he begin now?

(2.) He usually gave more than was prayed for. "He asked life of you, and you gave it to him, even length of days forever and ever" (Ps. 21:4). So to Solomon, God gave not only wisdom but riches and honor (I Kings 3:9-18). Abraham prayed for one son, and God gave him many by Hagar, Sarah, and Keturah. David desired one thing (Ps. 27:4), and God granted his request plus a kingdom, dominion, and glory. Jacob desired nothing except safety, food, and to return to the land of promise in peace, but the Lord added plenty to safety, having brought him back with great abundance and a company of people. "If God will be with me, and will keep me in the way that I go, and will give me bread to eat, and raiment to put on, then the Lord will be my God" (Gen. 28:20). There is his vow, his desire. See his return. "I went over the Jordan with this staff, and now I have become two bands" (Gen. 32:10). If the Lord will give more than is prayed for, then surely, faith may say, he will at least give as much as is prayed for. The Lord is not less bountiful now than in former times. His ear is not straightened nor his hand shortened. His ear is open to hear, and his hand is open to reward.

(3.) Prayer procured greater things in former times than any of you now have occasion to ask. It wrought miracles and that may be ascribed to faith in prayer (Heb. 11:33-35). This, as handled by Elijah, was the key of heaven which he opened when and how he pleased (James 5:17, 18). Prayer preserved Daniel in the midst of devouring lions; the opening of his mouth did shut theirs. Prayer brought Jonah out of the midst of the sea, out of the belly of a whale, safe on shore. Prayer revoked the sentence of death passed on Hezekiah, caused the sun to go backward, and brought an angel from heaven to destroy Sennacherib's host. Prayer ruined an army of ten hundred thousand and made them fly and fall before Asa (II Chron. 4:12). Prayer drew out the Lord's hand, destroyed Jehoshaphat's enemies by their own hands, armed them against themselves, and ruined them without his help (II Chron. 20). Prayer brought light into a dungeon, an angel from heaven into a prison, broke off chains, and opened iron gates (Acts 12:5-7). Did it work miracles in former times, and will it not procure ordinary mercies now? Is it less effectual? Does the Lord less regard it or love us less?

(4.) God heard his ancient people not only for themselves, but for others, for those whom he would not hear praying for themselves—for unbelievers and the most abominable of sinners—and that not only for one, or a few, but for whole cities, whole nations. He heard Abraham for Abimelech, a heathen prince in whose territories there was no fear of God. The Lord told him this (Gen. 20:7), and he was as good as his word (ver. 17). How often did he hear Moses for a whole nation in high rebellion against God! Even in the height of his fury, God appeased Moses. He heard Abraham for five cities, the most abominable that were to be found on the earth (Gen. 18:28-33). Abraham made six motions for the Sodomites, and the Lord rejected not one, condescending even to astonishment. We might think it had been wonderful if the Lord had but yielded to the first, yet to save five whole cities destined to destruction if there had been in them but fifty righteous persons? Further yet, so prevalent is prayer that the Lord yielded to save five cities for ten men (verse 32). Now if the Lord will hear his people for others, will he not hear when I pray for myself? If he would hear prayers for heathens, rebels, idolaters, and Sodomites, will he not hear me who is in covenant with him, justified by him, obedient to him, approved of him?

Obj. But does not the church complain, "O Lord God of hosts, how long will you be angry with the prayer of your people?" (Ps. 80:4). "When I cry and shout, he shuts out my prayer" (Lam. 3:8).

Ans. This may be misapprehension, thinking the Lord is angry when he is not. Zion complained, "The Lord has forsaken," but the Lord convinced her it was a mistake (Is. 49:14-16). They thought the Lord denied because he delayed, and they thought he was angry because he did not answer immediately; whereas delay itself is sometimes a gracious answer, a sign of love rather than anger. To bestow mercies when petitioners are unfit for them is to answer prayer in anger, but to defer till then is love. Their eyes may be so fixed on the particular desire as to take no notice of other prayers that are answered.

Consider his providence. This affords many encouragements to faith in prayer.

(1.) God hears those who cannot pray and answers that which cannot be called a prayer. He hears irrational creatures and listens to their cries though they lack both matter and form of praying. He rewards their very looks, answers their expectations, and fulfills their desires though they do not nor cannot properly be said either to look up to him or to wait on him or to desire him. "The young lions roar after their prey and seek their meat of God" (Ps. 104:21). "These all wait upon you that you may give them their meat in due season. You open your hand" (Ps. 104:27). "They are filled with good" (Ps. 104:28). "He gives to the beast his food, to the young ravens that cry" (Ps. 147:9). "The eyes of all wait upon you, and you give them meat in due season. You open your hand and satisfy the desire of every living thing" (Ps. 145:15, 16). They do but open their eyes, and God opens his hand. They do but intimate a natural desire by crying and looking, and God satisfies.

Now faith may say, "Does God care for oxen? Or does he say it altogether for our sakes? For our sakes, no doubt, that he who prays should pray in faith" (I Cor. 9:9). Will the Lord hear lions and ravens, and will he not hear me? Will he satisfy their natural desires and not my spiritual desires? Will he regard when their eyes are lifted up and not regard the lifting up of my heart? Am I not much better than they, being made in his image and being redeemed by the blood of his Son? It is Christ's own argument to strengthen faith (Mat. 6:26). Shall he not much more hear me (ver. 30)? He that will doubt here may well pass for one that has little faith. It is very weak if this will not support it.

(2.) He grants some things to men that they do not pray for. How much more will he grant what they do pray for!? "I was found by them that sought me not" (Is. 65:1). "Before they call, I will answer" (Is. 65:24). Some things, nay, the greatest things are granted to those who did not pray for them. No prayer had any influence in election, and our prayers contributed nothing to the glorious work of redemption. These fountains of mercy were dug without the help of any prayer. The greatest, sweetest streams of love ran freely before our prayers could draw them out. Regeneration, justification, pardon, adoption, and reconciliation are bestowed on those who cannot and who will not pray for them. For we cannot sincerely desire these before they are given. And how many other mercies, which we do not think of before we enjoy them, does he grant! Much precious fruit falls into our laps before we shake the tree by prayer. It may be they were the issue of someone else's prayers but not ours. Now if the water of life flows in such streams upon us when we do not pray, how pleasantly will they flow when they are drawn by the attractive power of prayer! If the Lord is found when we seek him not, opens when we knock not, and answers when we call not, how much more will he open and answer when we knock and call! If the greatest gifts are vouchsafed before we have hearts to pray, how confident may we be that prayer will obtain the less!

(3.) He makes some kind of returns to the prayers of unbelievers. He heard the voice of Ishmael (Gen. 21:17-18) and of Ahab, the most abominable of all the twenty kings of Israel. Now if they be heard in any sense—they who hated God and were hated of him, they whose prayers were as the howlings of dogs, to whom God was in no way engaged, who had none to intercede, none to help their infirmities, and no promise—how much more will he hear those who are his servants and have an interest in the intercession of Christ?

Consider your own experiences, how many times God has answered your prayers formerly. That will be a great encouragement to trust him for time to come. Those who have tried God through prayer are inexcusable if they will not trust him. His word is a sufficient ground for faith in prayer, but experience, withal, should exclude all doubting. This should both encourage us to pray and believe. David made this use of it. "Because he has inclined his ear unto me, therefore, I will call upon him as long as I live" (Ps. 116:2). Those who know what it is to enjoy communion with God in prayer and who frequently and fervently pray must have many experiences of sweet returns. It may be you have been afflicted in conscience, and by crying to God, you have found comfort as David (Ps. 116). Or in doubts and perplexities you found, "I cried to God, and he inclined toward me" (Ps. 116:2). Or in wants and necessities, "He supplied me." Or in fear and dangers, "He delivered me." Or in trouble and affliction, "He supported me, relieved me, and sanctified it to me." Or under temptation, being buffeted by Satan, "His grace was sufficient for me." Or when assaulted with some strong lusts, "He subdued them and strengthened me." Or when very desirous of some blessing, "He bestowed it on me." Now faith should argue from these experiences, "The Lord has heard me formerly, and why should I doubt that he will hear me now? He is the same God still, and prayer is as prevalent as acceptable. My person and services were unworthy then, and this did not hinder; therefore, it will not now." Paul's faith grew confident from former experiences. "The Lord stood with me and strengthened me" (II Tim. 4:17). There is his experience. See what inference his faith makes. "The Lord shall deliver me from every evil work" (II Tim. 4:18). So David (I Sam. 7:34-37). In like manner, we should conclude that because the Lord has heard me so frequently, so freely, so graciously, notwithstanding all my failings, weaknesses, and unworthiness, therefore, I will believe that he will hear me still, and he will answer me for time to come.

Limit not yourselves, nor the Lord, to the particular desire. You may pray in faith though you are not confident that the very thing desired shall be granted; for if you apprehend that this is the only way to pray in faith, you will neglect other ways. Since this particular confidence is sometimes required, you will sometimes pray in faith whereas this is always required. To prevent this, consider that there are divers acts which faith may put forth in prayer, any of which, in its season, will make the duty a prayer of faith.

(1.) We may pray in faith sometimes determinately, or if the word is not too bold, peremptorily. Faith may so act when you pray for things absolutely necessary for God's glory and your salvation. So you may ask in faith for temporal and spiritual blessings (as without which you cannot honor God or be serviceable in your callings) and be confident of receiving them.

Or when the Lord promises peremptorily and absolutely, faith is to keep proportion with the promise. If he promises absolutely, we may believe absolutely that we shall receive, such as "I will never leave you, nor forsake you" (Heb. 13:5). He promises peremptorily, so we desire that he would not forsake us, and we believe we shall be heard in this determinately. He says absolutely, "Having loved his own, he loved them to the end" (John 13:1). So we may pray that he would love us with an everlasting love, and we believe that he will hear us in this particular.

Or when he promises conditionally but has made you partakers of the condition, you may be said to pray in faith. "He that believes and is baptized shall be saved" (Mark 16:6). If he has given faith, you may pray for salvation and believe that he will hear, *i.e.*, he will save. "He that confesses and forsakes his sins shall have mercy" (Prov. 28:18). If he has enabled you to confess and forsake your sins in judgment, affection, and practice, you may pray for and expect to find mercy. So Matthew 5:4, if you mourn, you may pray for comfort and believe that you shall receive it.

(2.) We may pray in faith indefinitely, that is, when you believe your prayer shall be heard without pitching upon any particular way, time, or kind. He may be said to pray in faith who believes his person and prayer shall be accepted, though faith does not expect a particular answer. This has place when the promise is indefinite and a mercy is promised under a general notion without defining the way, time, manner, or kind in which it shall prove a mercy to me. So Romans 8:28, "All things work together for good to them that love God, to them who are the called according to his purpose." If you pray that such an occurrence or dispensation may work for good and believe that it shall, though you are not confident that it shall happen in such a manner, time, way, and degree, you still pray in faith. So Isaiah 3:10, "Say to the righteous that it shall be well with him." If you pray it may go well in every condition, and believe it shall, you shall receive a suitable answer. So Joel 2:32, "Whoever shall call on the name of the Lord shall be delivered." Though you do not believe that you shall be delivered at such a time, in such a manner, by such means, yet if in general you are confident of deliverance, you shall have it.

(3.) We may pray in faith disjunctively. To do so is to believe that you shall receive what you pray for or something better in reference to God's glory and your happiness. This is sufficient when you are not certain whether what you pray for is best for you. I say not whether it seems best, but whether it is best. In this case, it is not required that you should believe determinately that you shall receive what you pray for, but disjunctively, either this or something else which is better. In such a condition was Paul. "I am hard-pressed between the two, having a desire to depart and be with Christ, which is far better; nevertheless, to abide in the flesh is more necessary for you" (Phil. 1:23-24). When you are in such a straight, you may pray for what you apprehend to be best without believing that you shall be heard in that precisely, trusting God will answer either in that way or some other way.

(4.) We may pray in faith conditionally. We are to pray for nothing but what is commanded or promised, and the things we are to pray for are held forth in the Word with two sorts of conditions, some annexed to the promise and some annexed to the thing promised. Spiritual blessings are conditional because sometimes conditions are annexed to the promises whereby God engages himself to give them. Now, when he has already wrought the conditions, we may pray in faith for them absolutely, as before. When the conditions are not wrought, then we should pray for the conditions themselves, such as to "hunger and thirst after righteousness" (Mat. 5:10) and to "be faithful unto death" (Rev. 2:10). Temporal blessings are conditional because conditions are annexed to the things themselves, and they are such as these: if it seems good, if it is your will, if it is for your glory, if it is for my soul's good. Temporal favors are to be asked in faith, but faith must act conditionally. The like is to be observed concerning the removal of afflictions and vouchsafing of spiritual favors that tend to our well-being; faith in asking these must be acted, but acted conditionally and with submission. An example we have in David, a man strong in faith and much in prayer. "If I shall find favor in the eyes of the Lord, he will bring me again and show me both it and his habitation. But if he thus says, 'I have no delight in you,' behold, here I am, let him do to me as seems good unto him" (II Sam. 15:25-26). The faith of Christ, himself, acted conditionally. "If it is possible, let this cup pass from me. Nevertheless, not as I will, but as you will" (Mat. 26:39).

Chapter 5

How to Pray in Faith

Without faith it is impossible to please God. For he who comes to God must believe that he is and that he is a rewarder of those who diligently seek him.
Hebrews 11:6

NOW that you are grounded in the foundation of prayer—the intercession of Christ, the assistance of the Spirit, and the willingness of the Father to hear—you have every reason to pray in faith. Yet, what does it mean to pray in faith? To answer this, we must detail some necessary conditions and essential ingredients.

1. The asker must be in the faith, or rather, faith must be in him. The petitioner must be a believer. How can he ask in faith who has no faith? How can he ask in Christ's name who believes not in him? There is no audience, no answer for him that is not a believer. "God does not hear sinners" (John 9:31). Those who live in sin, live not by faith; or if you do not live in sin as to visible practice, yet sin lives in you, being entertained, loved, and condoned in the heart, you are not living by faith. When there is no faith, there will be no audience with God. "If I regard iniquity in my heart, the Lord will not hear me" (Ps. 66:18). God will not hear and answer that which displeases him. Prayer without faith does not please him; it is impossible that it should, for "without faith it is impossible to please God. For he who comes to God must believe that he is and that he is a rewarder of those who diligently seek him" (Heb. 11:6). God will not accept the service of prayer till the person is accepted

(Heb. 11:4). Abel obtained the witness that he was righteous and then God received his gifts. He obtained both by faith.

2. The thing asked for must be an object of faith, such as you may, upon good grounds, believe that God will grant. There must be a persuasion that the thing desired is lawful according to his will. "And this is the assurance that we have in him, that if we ask anything according to his will, he hears us" (I John 5:14). No request will he hear without assurance that what we ask is according to his will. Now, his will is that for which we have a biblical command or promise. In contrast, his decreeing or secret will does not belong to us; it is not the rule of our practice in prayer. Biblical examples may direct and encourage this act of faith in prayer, but it must be the example of the godly, approved, and ordinary. Extraordinary examples are not a rule for us, as that of David praying against particular enemies (Ps. 109); it is extraordinary since he had (as it is supposed) extraordinary assistance to discern that his particular enemies were incorrigible. Otherwise, though it may be lawful to pray against the public enemies of God or against the cause and practices of particular enemies, yet it is not lawful to pray against their persons. If there is no persuasion that the prayer is of faith, then it is sin; for whatever is not of faith is sin (Rom. 14:23), and sin cannot expect a comfortable return from God. He that cannot behold it will not hear it, or he will hear it so as to reward it with punishment. A fervent prayer for a thing unlawful is a crying sin.

3. The manner of asking must be faithful. It must be *in fide* (in faith) as to the person, *defide* (of faith) as to the object, and *fideliter* (faithfully) as to the manner. As he must be *bonus* (good) that asks and that which is asked must be *bonum* (good), so he must ask this *bene* (well) in three particulars.

(1.) *With fervency.* He does not ask in faith who does not ask fervently. "The effectual, *fervent* prayer of a righteous man avails much" (James 5:16). And that prayer is, according ver. 15, "the prayer of faith." It must be an inwrought prayer, proceeding from the powerful working of the Spirit in the heart. Now what the workings of the Spirit are in the heart as to prayer the apostle tells, "sighs that cannot be uttered" (Rom. 8:26). Such prayers show the person to be filled with the Holy Spirit and moved by him. Prayers must be strivings. "Strive together with me in your prayers" (Rom. 15:30). He that will prevail in prayer must wrestle with God like Jacob. Give the Lord no rest, as Isaiah 62:7 says. Cold, heartless prayers argue want of faith and will lack success; they teach God to deny. If there is only lip-labor, God will withdraw. If we pray as if we prayed not, God will hear as though he heard not, taking little notice except to correct us. Strong cries reach and pierce heaven; such were Christ's.

(2.) *With submission.* We must not limit God. To limit the Holy One of Israel is to tempt him, and that is a notorious effect of unbelief (Heb. 3:9, 12; 11:18). We must not limit God as to time, place, persons, things, or degrees.

Time. Be willing to wait God's time. He who believes makes not haste. It was an unbelieving prince that said, "Why should I wait on the Lord any longer?" God's Word says, "The vision is for an appointed time; though it tarries, wait for it" (Hab. 2:3-4).

Place. Jacob would not have prayed in faith for provision if he was unwilling to have it in Egypt.

Persons. Noah would not, in faith, have asked blessings for Ham if he had limited God as to the person. We must leave the Lord to his own way of free dispensation.

Things. Lawful things are temporal or spiritual. These are necessary for being (such as the means of grace) and for well-being (such as joy, assurance, and enlargements).

Temporal blessings must be desired with the conditions to which they are promised, and besides, with reference to God's good pleasure and caution of their expediency for us; namely, if it seems good to the Lord and if it is good for us. Spiritual blessings are to be sought for well-being since they are worth more than temporal blessings and since they are more expressly promised. But spiritual blessings necessary to salvation may be desired absolutely without reserve, conditions, or exceptions because they are so promised, and we are so commanded.

Degrees. We must not limit God to the degrees of grace or plenty or plausibleness of the means but refer to his infinite wisdom to bestow what degree he knows will make us most serviceable and what kind of means he pleases to make effectual for attaining those degrees.

(3.) *With right intentions.* It is not *bene* (well) except it is *ad bonum* (good). "You ask and do not receive because you ask amiss" (Jms. 4:8). We must pray to glorify God by being made serviceable to him and capable of communion with him. We must not desire grace to excel others, or as Simon Magus, we must not seek the Spirit to be admired and praised. We must not desire gifts to advance our credit and get applause, and we must not desire riches to satisfy our lusts and live at ease. This is to ask amiss; he that asks amiss must miss an answer.

These are the necessary conditions of this duty. I call them conditions because we cannot pray in faith without them, yet we may have these without praying in faith.

What is it to pray in faith? He whose faith puts forth any one of the following acts *prays in faith.*

1. *Particular application of a Scripture promise.* This is believing the promise whereby God has engaged himself to give what he asks. So to ask in faith is to pray with confidence that the Lord will grant the petition because he has promised. It is to pray with David, "Do good to your servant" and to rest assured that he will do it because it is his word and his promise (I Kings 8:24-26).

2. *Dependence upon God's mercy.* This is to cast one's self upon God without a specific promise, depending on him to grant the request. Faith in prayer supports itself upon God when there is no particular promise of the thing asked or when faith is so weak that it cannot make use of the promise by way of application. There are other supports of faith besides a promise and other acts of faith besides applying a promise which the soul putting forth in prayer may be said to ask in faith, and this act of dependence is one in particular. Faith can read an answer to prayer in the name of God and stay itself there when a promise does not appear or through faith's weakness cannot support it (Isaiah 1:10, 11).

3. *A general persuasion that the prayer shall be heard.* I call it general to distinguish it from that particular persuasion that the thing asked shall be presently granted, or granted at all, which is not simply necessary to this duty. The prayer may be heard, though the thing desired is not presently bestowed or bestowed at all. And so a man may pray in faith though he is not confident that what he prays for shall be given him. Zachariah prayed in faith, and it is likely he prayed when he was young, though the mercy which he asked was not granted till he was old (Luke 1:18). Noah prayed that God would persuade Japheth to dwell in the tents of Shem, yet this was not granted till many hundred years later. Christ prayed in faith that the cup might pass from him. It did not pass, yet his prayer was heard (Heb. 5:7). Paul prayed in faith that he might be free from that messenger of Satan. The mercy was not granted, yet his prayer was heard and graciously answered, "My grace is sufficient for you" (II Cor. 12:9). A prayer may be heard even though the mercy is not granted. Therefore, it is not necessary to this duty that a man should have a special persuasion to receive what he asks. He prays in faith who is persuaded in general that his prayer shall be heard, referring the answer to the wisdom and goodness of God to be returned when and how he pleases. He who believes God will hear his

prayer, though he is not confident that he will grant this particular desire, prays in faith.

4. *A special confidence that the request shall be granted.* This is the highest and rarest act of faith. If the desired mercy is temporal, it is extraordinary, raised in the heart by special intuition. It is now and then vouchsafed to those who are admitted to sweeter familiarity and nearer communion with God (Ps. 27).

Use. Take notice of the misery of unbelievers. They who cannot pray in faith must not expect to have their prayers heard. All men do not have faith, though most presume that they do. They cannot give an account how or when it was wrought, and they cannot show their faith by their works. Though they make many prayers, God will not hear. If this is your case, what will you do for support in distress, for supply of wants, for removal of fears and dangers? It is the great, sweet privilege of believers that whatever they ask in Christ's name, it shall be given. It is the misery of unbelievers that whatever they ask shall be denied or given in wrath. "Call upon me," says the Lord to believers, "in the day of trouble, and I will answer you" (Ps. 50:15). Unbelievers must read the contrary, "Though you call, I will not hear" (Pr. 1:28). To believers Christ says, "Ask, and it shall be given; seek, and you shall find; knock, and it shall be opened unto you" (Mat. 7:7). But to unbelievers he says, "Though you ask, I will not give." Christ says to them, as to the Jews, "You shall seek me but shall not find me, and where I go you shall not come" (Jn. 7:34). If they will not come to Christ, where will they go? Christ will neither hear them in life, nor at death, nor after death. Those who live in unbelief may read their doom. Those who die in unbelief will be sent to the gods they have served. He will say, "You would not come to me and believe in me that you might have life; therefore, you shall die in your sins, dying now and forever." After death, if you come with the foolish virgins and knock at the bridegroom's chamber, Christ will profess, "I know you not" and command a sad and everlasting departure.

Obj. The Ninevites prayed and were heard (Jonah 3:7, 8, 10). Ahab prayed and was heard (I Kings 21:27, 29). Both of them were unbelievers, Ahab notoriously so (ver. 25, 26).

Ans. As a prayer may be heard, yet the thing prayed for is not granted, so the thing desired may be granted, and yet the prayer is not heard. So it is with unbelievers. For, to speak strictly and properly, a prayer is not heard except when both person and prayer are accepted. No prayers are accepted but in Christ, and no prayers are in Christ but by faith. Therefore, unbelievers, both in respect to their person and prayers, are not accepted. Consequently, their prayers are not heard, though what they pray for might be granted, it is not out of respect to their prayer.

Ans. 2. The Lord gives nothing but temporal things upon the prayers of unbelievers. The Ninevites obtained a temporal deliverance, as did Ahab, receiving not a removal of the judgment threatened but a delay of its execution, and not forgiveness but forbearance. In the next generation, as some observe, Nineveh was quite destroyed, and the evil threatened to Ahab's family was fulfilled in his son's day. Unbelievers do not pretend to desire spiritual mercies, grace, regeneration, and holiness. No one desires these but those that have them in some degree.

Ans. 3. It is not in mercy when God gives temporal things to unbelievers who pray for them. Israel desired a king, and he gave them one in wrath. Israel desired meat, and he sent quails with his wrath upon them. Their pleasant meat had a bitter sauce (Ps. 106: 15; Num. 5:11, 88; Ps. 78:29-31). He gave them outward blessings but cursed them. Unbelievers, as such, have nothing in mercy. That is cursed which does not bring a soul-blessing with it. The only prayer that is properly heard is when mercy is the return of it.

Obj. If the Lord will not hear, why should we pray?

Ans. 1. We are obliged to obedience, though we are not assured of any reward. Subjection to God is necessary, being founded in our natures as his creatures. Reward is arbitrary as being grounded merely on his will which moves freely. Though God does not hear, we are bound to pray, for he has commanded it.

Ans. 2. Though unbelievers sin in praying, and therefore God will not hear them, yet they sin worse in not praying at all. It is a more heinous sin not to pray than not to pray in faith. A total omission is a greater abomination than an undue performance. It is much worse to fail in the substance than in the manner only.

Ans. 3. It is more dangerous not to pray at all than to pray amiss. The danger is proportional to the heinousness of the sin. He may deny mercy to those that pray amiss, but he will pour wrath on those who do not pray at all (Jer. 10:25).

Use 1. Exhortation to practice this duty: "Whatever you do, ask; whenever you ask, ask in faith." Nothing is more necessary than prayer, and no qualification of prayer is more necessary than faith. Of all duties and privileges, none is more advantageous and comfortable than prayer, but it must be faithful prayer. For without faith, there is neither advantage by it nor comfort in it. To pray without faith is to profane the ordinance. It is to take God's name in vain. Pray as often as you will, yet if not in faith, you will lose your labor. The apostle is peremptory: "Let not that man think he shall receive anything of the Lord" (James 1:7).

Use 2. For examination, test whether you pray in faith. It is a work of great importance. For if you do not pray in faith, it is a sign you have no faith; then you are under the law, cut off from Christ, exposed to the curse, and liable to eternal wrath. What is hell but abiding wrath? If you have faith but do not exercise it in prayer, you deprive yourselves of the benefit of this ordinance. Prayer is the conduit-pipe appointed by God to convey all the blessings of the upper and lower springs to the children of men, but if the passage is obstructed, it will be of no advantage to you. Lack of faith is a dangerous obstruction. This will hinder the passage of all mercy. Not a drop of the water of life will be conveyed by prayer without faith. Therefore, there is great reason to examine your faith.

(1.) Backwardness to pray is a sign that you do not pray in faith. He that believes he shall have whatever he asks, without upbraiding, will be ready and forward to ask upon all occasions. If you believed, you would omit no opportunity to address yourselves to God this way. You would not neglect it in your families, in secret, or in public. Those who omit it undervalue it, make no great account of it, spend whole days without it, and count it a burden saying, "What a weariness is prayer!" Those who take no pleasure or delight in prayer but come to it as a task cannot be said to pray in faith.

(2.) Carelessness in praying is a sign that you do not pray in faith. Prayer is a blessed engine, which, being carefully managed by faith, will procure all the mercies you need for time and eternity. If you believed this, you would not be so negligent in prayer but would stir yourself up to pray diligently. Those who pray only with their lips draw near only with their mouths. They make it only an exercise of the body, allowing their thoughts to wander without control, praying as if they prayed not. If you prayed in faith, you would observe the condition of such a prayer, one of which is fervency. Where luke-warmness, indifference, formality, and distractions are tolerated, faith is not exercised.

(3.) On the contrary, perplexity and solicitousness removed after prayer is a sign that you pray in faith. Take Hannah for an example (I Sam. 1). Though she spoke out of the abundance of her complaint and grief, yet afterward, her countenance was no more sad. Faith is expressed by casting our burden upon the Lord. He who groans and is oppressed under a burden is relieved when he is able to lay it upon another. Likewise, he that puts forth faith in prayer casts his burden upon God. Therefore, after such a prayer, the oppressed soul will be at ease and "return to its rest."

(4.) Are God's promises your encouragement in prayer? Do they draw you to pray? Do they quicken you while praying? Do they encourage you to expect a return after prayer? Do you plead the Word? Do you urge the promise? Then it is faith. Thus, the people of God have done in their prayers of faith, such as Moses (Num. 14:17, 18), Solomon (I Kings 8:23-26), and David (Ps. 119:25, 28, 58, 65, 76, 116). Do you plead the word of promise: "Though I am unworthy to be heard, yet you, O Lord, are worthy to be honored. It is not for your honor to neglect your word. Though I can do nothing to engage you, yet you have engaged yourself, and you will be true to your engagements. Though nothing is due to me but wrath, yet you have made mercy due to me by your promise; therefore, I will expect it. You will not detain what you yourself have made due. Though I forget my promises and resolutions for you, yet you will not forget your covenant. It is your attribute as 'a covenant-keeping God,' and though you may deny me, yet you will not deny yourself." Does the faithfulness and righteousness of God encourage you to ask and expect an answer? Do you plead these truths and promises as David did? Do you plead: "Deliver me in your righteousness" (Ps. 119:40; 143:1)? Do you plead, "Though my unrighteousness testifies against me, yet the Lord is righteous from everlasting to everlasting. Is it not a righteous thing with the Lord to do what he has said? Though I am unfaithful and have dealt falsely in the covenant, yet my unfaithfulness cannot make God's faithfulness of no effect. The Lord has promised, and faithful is he who has promised, who also will do it." To conclude, to act upon the righteousness and faithfulness of God engaged in the promise is the work of faith. The prayer where such actings are found is a prayer of faith. Where the promise raises the heart to hope, hope quickens it to more frequency and more fervency in prayer.

(5.) Can you submit to the Lord's time for an answer, believing that your prayer shall either be answered now or hereafter when it is best for you? This is enough to denominate your prayers. Faith is a submissive grace; it will not prescribe to the Lord nor limit the Holy One. It will acknowledge him both Lord of what he gives and of the time when he will give it. Sometimes the Lord answers presently (Gen. 24:12-15; Dan. 9). Sometimes "the vision is for an appointed time, though it tarries, we must wait for it" (Hab. 2:3). So do those who live (and pray) by faith (Hab. 2:4). It is uncertain to us when the appointed time is, whether now or hereafter. "It is not for us to know the times and the seasons" (Acts 1:7). So Christ told his disciples when they were a little too peremptory as to a present answer, "It is not for you to know" and commanded them to wait (Acts 1:4). Faith will be content to act upon what God has revealed. It is unbelief that pries into God's secrets. Faith will be content with God's time. It is unbelief that would confine the Lord to our time. "He that believes makes not haste" (Is. 28:16). He will stay God's leisure, entrusting himself to him who knows what time is best. It is unbelief that is so hasty. Unbelief must have it now or not at all (II Kings 6:33). It is sufficient to form a prayer of faith, believing the Lord will answer either in our time or his, either now or hereafter, and to rest satisfied with this. If faith acts this way in prayer, you pray in faith.

(6.) Are you persuaded that the Lord will give either what you desire or what is better? Do you rest in this truth, that you shall have what you ask either in kind or in equivalency, and that the Lord will satisfy your desires either as to the letter of your petition or to the intention of it? Do you acquiesce in this, that the Lord will answer you either according to your will or according to his, that he will give either what you think is best or what he thinks is best? Do you believe that he will give either what you desire or what is better than what you desire? If so, you pray in faith.

It is a great mistake to think that you do not pray in faith unless you believe the very particular request shall be granted which you ask. Faith acts in a greater latitude, has a larger sphere, and reaches as far as that providence which orders the returns of prayer. Faith acts for an answer since the Lord is accustomed to make answers. Now, it is clear in Scripture and experience that the Lord answers not only by giving the thing desired but by vouchsafing something else as much or more desirable. The disciples asked, "Will you restore the kingdom?" (Acts 1:6). They desired a temporal kingdom. God did not gratify them in this, yet he granted that which was much better: "You shall receive power when the Holy Spirit has come upon you, and you shall be my witnesses" (Acts 1:8). As faith is not confined in such narrow bounds, it will not limit the Holy One of Israel. To limit the Lord is to tempt him, and to tempt God is an act of unbelief. By this the Israelites provoked God in the wilderness (Ps. 78:41). This is censured under the notion of unbelief. It was from their unbelief that they limited God. They were not contented with manna (though angels' food) which the Lord thought best for them. They wanted flesh, too. They had to have meat or nothing. Their lusting was a peremptory desire; it was an issue of unbelief. We may judge the nature of this desire by the quality of the answer. If it had been a desire of faith, it would have been an answer in mercy, but the Lord answered them in wrath (Ps. 78:29-31). He gave them their own desire since they would not be satisfied, but they had the wrath of God with it. The Lord does not answer the desires of faith in this manner. They are of another strain. They will be satisfied either with what is desired or with what the Lord counts better. It is unbelief that must have that which is desired or nothing. Faith is not so dictatorial. When we pray for things not absolutely necessary or comparatively necessary, we may pray in faith though we do not believe that the particular desire shall be granted. It is sufficient in these cases if we believe the Lord will either vouchsafe that or something else which he knows to be better. Therefore, if your faith acts accordingly in prayer, it may be called a prayer of faith.

(7.) Can you suspend your hopes of an answer upon a condition, upon such conditions as have warrant and approbation in Scripture? Faith acted conditionally is enough, in some cases, to constitute a prayer of faith. Abraham prayed in faith, yet his prayer ran in a conditional strain (Gen. 18:29, 30, 32). So Solomon (I Kings 8:35, 44, 47) and Christ himself (Luke 22:42) prayed likewise. The apostle John mentioned a conditional confidence (I John 5:14). The confidence is that he will hear when we ask. The condition is if we ask according to his will, which comes to the same issue, if we ask what is good for us; for what is good for us is according to his will.

In case you are uncertain what is according to his will, if he has not absolutely manifested by command, promise, or something equivalent that what you desire is his will, or in case you are uncertain whether what you pray for be absolutely good for you, in these cases, when you believe that what you pray for shall be granted, if it is according to his will, or if it is best for you, you pray in faith; no more is required. Augustine gave this rule for regulating our prayers as to temporal things, and it applies to spiritual mercies when there is that uncertainty now spoken of: "Ask with restriction, conditionally, leaving it to him to give if it is good or to deny if it is hurtful, submitting your will and wisdom to him."

Chapter 6

How to Recognize God's Answers to Our Prayers

❧

I will watch to see what he will say to me.
Habakkuk 2:1

IF you entertain such thoughts that God has denied or rejected your petitions, you may be apt to fear he will do so for time to come. Such fears and suspicions are as worms at the root or as a palsy in the hand of faith, depriving it of strength and steadfastness. They are as storms which unsettle, shock faith, and make it waver as a wave of the sea. This must be removed as it is inconsistent with that confidence which the Lord expects in all that approach him. To remove it, consider that the Lord may answer your prayers when you take no notice of it. He has many ways to answer our petitions, whereas we ordinarily take notice of just one, and if the answer comes not that way, we conclude there is no answer and thereby wrong the Lord and ourselves. We may think he does not hear when he both hears us and answers us. Take notice how many ways God may answer your prayer, and you will see many more reasons to conclude that he granted all, though you did not observe how.

1. Prayer is answered even when there is no visible effect of it. Prayer is not in vain if the person is accepted and the service approved. Do you think it is nothing to please God, to do that in which his soul delights, to offer that which ascends to him as the fragrance of a sweet aroma? Is it nothing to obey God, to honor him, to give a testimony to his glorious perfections by praying? Is it nothing to be admitted to such sweet, intimate communion with God in such a familiar way so as to speak with him as a man to his

friend, as a child to his father? Suppose you should reap no other benefit by prayer, is not this as much as will amount to an answer? If you will not measure the return of your prayers by lower inferior advantages, these are the most blessed returns. It should be more desirable in your account to please him than to be happy yourselves. His glory should be more valuable than your salvation or all the means that tend to it. Such society with him should be esteemed the first-fruits of heaven. Yet these are the privileges of every accepted prayer; therefore, if it is accepted, though it obtains nothing more, it is abundantly answered.

2. God sometimes makes prayer an answer to itself and answers when you are praying. "While they are yet speaking, I will hear" (Is. 65:24). He not only hears but answers the prayer by enabling us to pray (Dan. 9:20, 21). While Daniel was speaking in prayer, an angel was sent in answer to his desires. You will judge this as a sweet return. But how much more is it for the Holy Spirit to be sent into the heart and thereby to have powerful assistance, comfortable enlargements, heavenly affections, and vigorous exercise of graces; to have the soul winged with holy affections, to fly into the bosom of Christ and to have heaven, as it were, opened and the veil withdrawn that the light of God's countenance may break out and shine upon the soul! These are the greatest, the sweetest of spiritual blessings which infinitely transcend all outward enjoyments (Ps. 4:6-8). Well, then, may they be accounted most blessed answers.

3. God sometimes answers prayer by revealing the defects of prayer such as formality, luke-warmness, unbelief, carelessness, sloth, irreverence, hypocrisy, self-seeking, or whatever else may render their prayer offensive. If sins are discovered while praying, it is a great advantage and mercy; and if it obtains so much as to just reveal this, surely, it is not unanswered.

4. It is an answer to prayer, and a gracious answer at that, to sometimes be denied. You consider it a good answer to a petition

when you have that which is better than the thing desired, but when you desire that which is not good, the denial is better than the grant. The denial is a mercy; the grant would be a judgment. So it was with David. He was importunate for the life of his child, but it was better for him that the Lord did not grant its life since it would have been a living monument of his ignominy wherein every beholder might have read both his shame and heinous sin. The Lord is oftentimes merciful in denying outward blessings and worldly enjoyments to his children. He denies them plenty of temporals lest they should bring leanness to their souls. He denies them health that their souls may prosper. He denies comfort in dearest relations by making them cross and uncomfortable lest they should steal away the heart from himself. These denials are great mercies and therefore sweet returns of prayer.

5. God sometimes answers prayer by bestowing only some degree of the thing desired, not the whole. The Lord answered Moses's prayer by giving him a view of Canaan, not the full possession. Those who pray for increase of grace are answered when the Lord draws out the heart in stronger desires after it. Desires after grace are a degree of grace. If the messenger of Satan, against which Paul prayed, was some corruption, then his prayer was answered, though not totally, but in some degree, so as to have sufficient power to resist. The prayers of God's people for the destruction of antichrist are answered in some degree in that the impostures of that man of sin are discovered, and so many nations fallen off; many hate her, though make her not desolate.

6. God may hear the prayer though he does not answer it presently. Delay is no denial. Prayer is sure to be heard though the Lord sometimes seems slow in granting what is prayed for. Delay is sometimes a mercy. He never defers when it is seasonable to grant. "The Lord is not slack, as some men count slackness" (II Pet. 3:9), or as though he had altered his purpose, forgotten his

promise, or was careless to accomplish it. He defers in mercy. He is not slack, though he may seem so to us (ver. 8). The promise was of the Day of Judgment, the coming of Christ, which is the prayer of the church (Rev. 10:20). As soon as it is seasonable, he will come instantly, not deferring one moment. As soon as it will be a mercy, "shall not God avenge his elect though he bears long with them? I tell you that he will avenge them speedily" (Luke 17:17). Stay long and yet speedily. He waits that we may exercise faith in prayer (Heb. 10:35). Christ prayed for his enemies and was answered after his resurrection. Stephen prayed for his persecutors and was answered after his death in Saul's conversion. How long did God's ancient people pray for the coming of the Messiah, and the primitive Christians for good magistrates, and all the faithful for the ruin of antichrist, and the primitive martyrs for vengeance against their persecutors? (Rev. 6:10). Prayers are seed that lie underground and talents that are laid up in heaven for improvement. One talent in prayer will be improved to ten in its return. Though the answer is as a cloud in your days, it may cover the heavens for your posterity and rain showers of blessings. The last times will be times of the greatest mercies because many answers are reserved for them. There is, therefore, no reason to conclude you are denied because you are not presently answered.

7. God may grant the mercy desired though not to the person for whom it is desired. He may answer your prayers by bestowing that on another which you desire for yourselves. So Moses was answered—he desired to conduct the Israelites into Canaan, but the Lord appointed a dear relation of his, Joshua, his servant, to be their conductor. Or God may bestow that upon you which you desire for others. For example, David's prayer returned to his own bosom (Ps. 35:13). The Lord will not allow prayer to be in vain. Abraham desired the promise to be accomplished in Ishmael, but the Lord fulfilled it in Isaac. Isaac desired the blessing to fall upon

Esau, but the Lord bestowed it on Jacob. What David desired for his first child by Bathsheba, God granted to the second child, Solomon. The apostles desired the benefits of the Messiah to principally be the portion of the Jews, but the Lord vouchsafed them to the Gentiles. There is no reason to conclude that he denies because he answers not as to the individual.

8. God answers by granting something else in lieu of what is desired, though he bestows not the same thing. He answers if he grants something as good or better. " 'Do you seek great things for yourself? Seek them not. For, behold, I will bring evil upon all flesh,' says the Lord, 'but your life will I give unto you' " (Jer. 45:5). It was better for Baruch to have his life where he was than to enjoy a plentiful estate where he would have no security of his life. God seldom or never denies the particular request, but he gives something as good or better, in one or all of these four respects.

First, he answers in kind. When we pray for temporals, he gives spirituals. The apostles desired Christ would rule as a temporal king, but God used them as his instruments to erect a spiritual kingdom. They desired outward preferment, to sit at his right or left in worldly pomp, but he assured them of spiritual and eternal glory, that they should sit upon twelve thrones.

Second, he answers in reference to the rule of goodness, which being *summi bona,* that which is agreeable must be best. That is best for us which pleases him most. If he does not make a return of our prayers according to our wills, yet he always does according to his will, and that, being the rule of goodness, is best for us.

Third, he answers in reference to the great end for which we pray, which is his glory. If he does not give the very thing desired, yet he will give something that will tend more to his glory, and that which most conduces to his glory is best, not only in respect of God but for us, because our chief happiness consists in his glory. The more we honor him, the greater is our happiness, and that is best, for sure, which makes us most happy. It is a sweet answer to prayer when he gives that which is better than what we desire.

Fourth, he answers in reference to the particular end of your desire. If he does not give the mercy desired, he will give something that will as much advance the end for which you desire it. And if you have the end for which you aimed at, you have your desires, for the means is not otherwise desirable. If you desire a blessing that you may live contentedly and he doesn't bestow that, he will bestow another mercy that will afford as much or more contentment. You desire an alteration of your condition that you may live more contentedly; if the Lord does not alter your condition but changes your heart, so as to make it contented with your present state, he gives that which is as good or better than what you desire and so has returned a sweet answer to your prayers. Or if your desires pitch upon some particular means to subdue a lust, though he does not grant it, yet if he offers another means which is more effectual to subdue that lust, he has granted what is as good or better. Or if you desire the removal of some affliction that you might with more liberty and cheerfulness serve the Lord, though he removes it not, yet if he enables you under that affliction to serve him with as much cheerfulness and enlargement of heart, then he has granted your request and has answered your prayers.

But some are discouraged by a sense of unworthiness. A humble soul will be apt to say, "How can I believe the Lord will hear me when I am so vile, not only in respect of the common condition of mankind, being but dust and ashes, a worm, less than a worm, but also being more than ordinarily sinful, having often profaned this ordinance and abused former comfortable returns? In respect of my condition in the world, being so low and contemptible as I cannot be confident of access to men of any extraordinary note in the world, how much less can I be confident of acceptance or audience with the great and holy God?" To remove this, consider:

(1.) The Lord never heard any that were worthy or accounted themselves so. All that ever had an audience with God have been unworthy in their own esteem. The Lord requires not that his people should bring any worth with them to commend their prayers to him. The want of personal worth never hindered the Lord from answering prayer. Therefore, there is no reason to be discouraged for lack of that which is neither necessary nor was ever present. No flesh is justified in his sight.

(2.) The more sensible we are of our own unworthiness, the more hope we have of an answer and acceptance. This is so far from being any just impediment to faith that it should rather encourage it, for Scripture and experience tell us that it is both the Lord's gracious disposition and practice to do most for those who are, or who reckon to themselves to be, most unworthy. "He fills the hungry" (Luke 1:38, 48) but "casts down the mighty" (ver. 52). He pronounces them blessed who are poor (Mat. 5:3). He calls not many wise and noble (I Cor. 1:26-28). He seeks that which is lost (Luke 6:19, 20). He saves sinners, the chief of them (I Tim. 1:15). He invites beggars, sending out his servants to fetch them (Luke 14:21, 23). He aids those who have no money and no worth (Isa. 40). He pities those whom no eye pities (Ezek. 16:6). He condescends to those who are lowest, taking pleasure in it and getting honor by it. Hereby are the freeness and the riches of his grace made more conspicuous; infinite mercy appears more merciful. Consider the different demeanor and success of the Pharisee and the publican as to this duty, and it will put it past doubt. Consider what self-confidence and conceitedness are in the one and what humility and sense of unworthiness are in the other. "This man went away justified rather than the other" (Luke 18:14). Justified meaning pardoned, accepted, and answered. He was justified and *not* the other. The reason is observable: "For everyone who exalts himself shall be humbled, and he who humbles himself shall be exalted." A sense of unworthiness should strengthen rather than discourage prayer.

(3.) Prayer and praying in faith are not only a privilege but a duty, and is anyone unworthy to do his duty? If it was only a privilege, unworthiness might be some plea to keep sinners from meddling with prayer or acting faith, but since it is a duty, you have no reason not to pray. What, are you unworthy to obey God, to do what he commands, to do as he requires? The very thought of this is absurd. Men would laugh at such a plea. God will be far from accepting it. Would you take it well from your servant if he should neglect to do what you command under the pretense that he is unworthy to obey you? Yes, you would count it a jeer. You would think him lazy and foolish in finding no better excuse for his idleness. The case is alike in reference to God. We are unworthy to receive but not to obey. There is no show of reason why this should be a discouragement.

(4.) Though you are unworthy to be heard, yet Christ is worthy. It is he who undertakes to present your petition and procure an answer. Believers, when they are found praying, are found as Paul, "not having their own righteousness, but that which is through the faith of Christ, that which is of God by faith" (Phil. 3:9). Faith makes Christ yours, and so his righteousness is yours. It unites you to Christ as to your head, *Caput et membra sunt quasi una mystica persona.* When the Lord looks on you, he finds you having Christ's righteousness, and that is enough to make both persons and prayers righteous, covering all unworthiness in either that might hinder acceptance. Though Christ does not transmit his merits, yet he transmits the efficacy and benefits of his merits to our account. He is worthy that we should be heard.

Others are discouraged by the weakness of their prayers. A humble soul will be apt to say, "I am not only unworthy, but my prayers are weak, much unlike the prayers of God's people formerly. My prayers are accompanied with many infirmities, deadness of heart, straightness of spirit, formality, and distractions." To remove this, consider:

(1.) You may mistakenly think your prayers are weak when they are strong. The strength of prayer does not consist in anything outward. It does not consist in expressions or tears or outward gestures and enlargements. It is a hidden, inward strength. Outward expressions may sometimes be the signs but never the sinews. Men may judge its strength by multitude of words or passion of expression, but the Lord sees not as man sees. Man looks on the outward appearance, but the Lord looks on the heart (I Sam. 16:7). Man's judgment differs far from God's. Man may judge something to be weak which God judges to be strong. The strength of prayer lies in the heart, in the motion of zeal and faith. Faith and fervency are the strength of prayer. Faith is principally, and fervency is as it springs from faith. All affections without faith will not prevail. Cut out faith, and you cut out the strength of prayer. For though zeal might be the most prevalent exercise on earth and has power both with God and men, yet without faith, it is like Samson deprived of his locks (Judges 16:17). Though a great champion of Israel, Samson's strength went from him, and he became weak like any other man. So prayer without faith becomes weak. You should not be discouraged from believing because your prayers are weak, but rather be persuaded to exercise faith that your prayers may be strong.

(2.) Examine whether those weaknesses are voluntary or involuntary. Examine whether they are through unavoidable infirmity or through voluntary carelessness, sloth, and negligence. If they are voluntary and you are content that it should be so; if you are slothful and will not stir up yourselves to lay hold on God; if you lack faith because you will not exercise it nor summon up spiritual forces of affection and graces to follow after God, then I confess your condition is sad and full of sin and discouragements.

So long as you continue to be slothful, the word affords little encouragement. You must pray if you would be heard and not pray as though you prayed not. You must cry if you would be answered, offering up strong cries. You must follow hard after God if you would find him. You must lay hold on him and stir up all your strength to do it if you would enjoy him. But if these weaknesses are involuntary, if you bewail and mourn for them; if they are your burden and affliction; if you long, thirst, and breathe after more strength of faith; if you earnestly endeavor to shake off these distempers and be diligent in the use of all appointed means to gather more strength to your prayers; then this mourning, longing, and endeavoring are signs that the Lord will not take notice of your infirmities. He will not charge your weaknesses upon you nor impute them to you. Rather, they shall not hinder the Lord from hearing and answering nor should they hinder you from believing. In these cases, the Lord accepts the will for the deed (II Cor. 8:12), answering and rewarding weak prayers as though they were strong. He stands not so much upon the quantity of your strength but the sincerity of your endeavors. He will look upon you and reward you, not according to what you are but according to what you would be. He that has but a little faith and puts it all out in prayer shall prevail more than he who prays with much faith but does not pray with all. This is plain from Christ's testimony of the widow (Luke 21:8). Her two mites were worth more than the twenty talents cast in by one who had a hundred. The Lord is so gracious that he will accept a little from those who cannot do much than accept much from those who can do more. He does not despise the day of small things but takes special notice of a little strength (Rev. 3:8). There is no reason, therefore, to be discouraged from weaknesses of faith in prayer if it is not voluntary.

(3.) If you are weak, labor to pray that your faith may be strong. This should rather be a motive than a discouragement. Would you think him reasonable who, being weak, would neglect or refuse nourishment because he is weak? He should rather receive it that he might become strong. So here, to act faith in prayer is the best way to get ability and strength to pray powerfully. Faith draws together both domestic and auxiliary forces, stirs up the strength of the soul, and engages the strength of Christ. Those who wrestle with that strength shall surely prevail. The efficacy of the head is divided into the body by means of the union between head and members. Now, it is faith that unites us to Christ. He who has all power in heaven and earth dwells in our hearts by faith, making his strength ours. The ancients through faith, "out of weakness were made strong" (Heb. 11:34), not only strong in battle to prevail against the armies, but strong in prayer to prevail with God. If you would be strong in prayer, you must pray in faith that your weaknesses may be scattered and your infirmities put to flight. These should not drive you from your confidence, but engage you to be confident, since this is the only way to grow strong.

Chapter 7

A Definition of Saving Faith

The just shall live by faith.
Romans 1:17

BEFORE we conclude, it is requisite to resolve some cases.

First, since it is necessary that those who would receive answers must pray in faith, that is, they must be confident and assured that their prayers shall be answered, what can they expect who lack assurance, who (as to their own apprehension) do not have the ground of this confidence? How can they be confident of this privilege when they are full of fears and doubts that they are not in that state of which this privilege is entailed? How can they pray in faith who fear they have no faith? How can they believe their prayers will be accepted who see no ground to believe that their persons are accepted? This is the case of those who, being in or newly past the pangs of the new birth, have the seeds of faith but not the evidence. Faith is in its infancy but not grown up to that maturity so as to know itself. Such walk in darkness and see no light. They have no light to discover that God is their Father, that the promise is their portion, that Christ intercedes for them, or that the Spirit intercedes through them. What support can these have in reference to the success of their prayers? This may be the case also of those who have had assurance but have now lost it; who are in that sad condition as they have occasion to invert the apostle's expression, that they were sometimes light in the Lord but now they are darkness. Their former evidence is blotted, their former light is clouded, and the Spirit of God is suspending their assurance and testimony either for trial or upon some provocation. The question here will be: What encouragement and support may such have as to the issue of their prayers? Can they pray in faith? Or can they pray so that their prayers shall be granted?

A faith of dependence may constitute a prayer of faith where assurance is wanting. Those who through the weakness of faith or the withdrawings of God in time of desertion are destitute of assurance may yet pray in faith if they exercise this faith of dependence. To open this a little, a faith of dependence believes God *may* answer; a faith of assurance believes God *will* answer. One says, "Probably the Lord will hear." The other says, "Certainly the Lord will hear." Jonathan went out against the Philistines in the strength of that faith we express by depending or relying upon God, and it rose no higher than, "It may be that the Lord will work for us" (I Sam. 14:6). Now, faith thus acted in prayer makes it a prayer of faith. But to resolve this case more fully and clearly, I shall endeavor to do four things:

(1.) To show that relying on God for an answer is sufficient to make a prayer of faith. It is this faith which justifies a sinner. The person being justified is accepted. If the person is accepted, then the prayer is accepted and will be answered. A sinner is not justified by assurance but by an act of dependence or relying on Christ. For he is justified by the first act of faith when he first believes. Assurance comes after the first act of believing (Eph. 1:18). The Spirit's work of assurance comes after believing. A faith of dependence without assurance is sufficient to render the prayer acceptable and capable of an answer. This relying, acted in prayer, makes it a prayer of faith. Besides, this faith is sometimes all that is required and all that is expressed in those prayers which have been graciously answered (Joel 2:12-14). The prophet Joel directed them how to address themselves to the Lord. Faith is necessary in all such addresses, yet all the faith whereby they made this address is in those words, "Who knows? He may turn and relent and leave a blessing" (Joel 2:14). It is no more than this: It may be the Lord will return and repent (Jonah 3:9). That faith, in the strength of sending up those mighty cries, goes no farther than a "maybe, who can tell?" Yet this prayer prevailed (Jonah 3:10). So it is clear from this that a faith of dependence, acted in prayer, will prevail with God for an answer and make it a prayer of faith.

(2.) I will show the objects upon which this faith is acted and by which it is supported, as well as how it is to be exercised on them in the cases propounded. The objects to which I will be confined at this time are three.

[1.] *The name of God.* The Lord directs those that are in darkness to this object: his name (Isa. 1:10). There is enough in his name to encourage and support the weakest and to silence all his fears and doubts as to the success of his prayers. See it declared (Exod. 34:6, 7). Here is firm footing for that faith which is so weak and small that it cannot be discerned by him that has it. It is said of Abraham that he "did not waver in unbelief" (Rom. 4:20). The reason is because he had firm footing for both feet. He that stands upon one leg may easily stagger. He that is persuaded that God is able but not willing, or willing but not able, stands upon one leg. But Abraham was persuaded of both the promise that God was willing and able, both being expressed in Romans 4:21. Therefore, his faith, having ground for both feet, stood sure and steadfast; it staggered not. Now the name of God affords good ground for faith. There is in it that which may persuade a doubting soul that God is both able and willing. "The Lord, the Lord God" in Hebrew is "Jehovah, Jehovah EL," the strong God. It means he that has his being of himself and gives being to things that are not. By his name, he shows that he is able to give being to all you want or desire. He is able to make you pray and able to make all desirable returns to your prayers, doing "above what you can ask or think." That he is willing, the rest of his name shows, for he is "merciful and gracious." He is merciful, and misery is a proper plea for mercy. Am I not miserable? He is gracious, and grace expects no motive from without. Free grace will move itself and will not be stopped by any hindrance from within. Unworthiness cannot hinder, for then it is most grace when it rests in the most unworthy. Am I not such a one? Long continuance in sin cannot hinder if it is broken off by repentance, for he is long-suffering. No, nor the abounding sinfulness of sin, for he is abundant in goodness. No, nor the infinite multitude and variety of sins, for he forgives iniquity, transgression, and sin. Nor the huge number of petitioners, for he keeps mercy for thousands. Though the doubting soul cannot plead his truth (another letter of his name) in reference to the covenant, as not knowing his interest in the covenant, yet he may plead it in reference to the declaration of his name. As sure as God is true, so sure is he merciful and gracious.

[2.] *The free offers of Christ.* The Scripture abounds with them. I will instance one. "All that the Father gives me shall come to me, and him that comes to me, I will in no wise cast out" (John 6:37). That which faith principally eyes in Christ for the success of prayer is his intercession, that is, his office as advocate. Now, though a doubting soul dares not rely upon Christ as one that is his advocate, yet he may rely on him as one that offers to be his advocate. He professes that he will in no wise refuse any that will come to him. The soul may say, "Christ prayed for his enemies, for those that were murdering him. May he not then also intercede for me? It is true that I have been an enemy, but oh, how I hate myself for that enmity! I have now laid down arms, and though I can do little for him, yet I resolve never more to oppose him, though I perish. Since he was so gracious as to pray for his murderers (Luke 23:34), who knows but he may intercede for me? Christ prayed not only for those who actually believed but for those who should afterward believe (John 17:20). He prayed for those who had no faith when he prayed." And is not this your case, poor doubting or deserted soul? Is not this the worst you can make of it? Can you say anything worse of yourself than, "I do not believe, and I have no faith"? Well, then, look to Christ and rely on him as one who intercedes for unbelievers, and hereby you will show you have faith and your prayers will be answered.

[3.] *The general promises* which the dark soul apprehends to be out of its reach, such as "He is a rewarder of them that diligently seek him" (Heb. 11:6) and "Whoever shall call on the name of the Lord shall be delivered" (Joel 2:32) may reason that there was nothing in man that could move the Lord to make these promises, and there is nothing in man that can hinder him from performing them when and where he pleases. And who knows but he may perform them to me? It is true, I have neglected Christ formerly, but now I resolve to seek him indeed. And though I am not certain that he will be found of me, yet I will seek him early, seek him first, seek him before all others, seek him principally, seek above all others, and who knows but I may, at last, find him? He has been found of those that sought him formerly. He has been found of those that sought him not. Will he not be found of me who seeks him?

(3.) The acts of this faith in which it is exercised and by which it may be discerned:

[1.] *Renouncing*. A renouncing of all supports and refuges but Christ. See it in repentant Ephraim. "We will no more rely on Assyria nor trust in our armies of horse" (Hos. 14:3). So the soul will rely no more on his own wisdom, righteousness, works, or performances. When he comes to pray, he will not ground his confidence on what he does, or what he is, or what he is not, as the Pharisee. He perceives these to be but a refuge of lies. Though he comes destitute and helpless and does not have much to assure him that God is his Father, yet here is his support in this orphan state, "In thee the fatherless find mercy" (Hos. 14:3).

[2.] *Submission.* A dependent soul will be content with anything if the Lord will but own him, if Christ will but smile on him. This is visible in the returning prodigal. "I will return to my father" (Luke 15:18, 19). There is faith. It is as if he says, "Though you have dealt with me as a father, yet I am unworthy to be called a son, unworthy to be entertained and employed as a son. Let me be anything so as I may have a being in your house. Let me come under your roof, and I will be content though I have no other usage, respect, or reward. The lowest office in your house is too good, only let me not be shut out of doors." The woman of Canaan, though she followed Christ with such strength of faith and importunity of prayer that evoked his admiration, yet she was so submissive that she would be content with crumbs or anything that has relation to children (Mat. 15:22; II Sam. 15:25).

[3.] *Acceptance.* He will yield to any terms so long as the Lord will grant his chief desires. When he hears that to have Christ he must forsake all and follow him, he embraces the motion saying, "This is a faithful saying and worthy of all acceptance" (I Tim. 1:15). He says with Mephibosheth, "Let him take all if my Lord will return to my soul in peace." If he wants to inherit the land of promise, he must come out of Egypt. All his lusts must go, small and great, secret and open, pleasant and profitable. His Zoars shall be turned into ashes. His Herodias and his pleasant beloved sins shall be divorced. The best and fattest of the cattle, his profitable and gainful sins, shall be put to the sword with the rest of the children of Amalek. His secret idols that are hidden shall not only be buried, but as Moses with the calf, they shall be ground to powder. Tell him that if he will be joined to Christ, he must forget his kindred and his father's house, his former old acquaintances and way of life. He is to be satisfied in the King so he will take delight in his beauty. Tell him, if he will have Christ as an intercessor, he must submit to him as a king. Oh, he says, if the golden scepter may be held forth,

I will submit to it forever. Tell him if he will have the Spirit of Christ, he must have him as a Spirit of grace as well as a Spirit of supplication. He must yield with cheerfulness, looking upon holiness as garments of gold that will enrich and beautify him. He must view the sanctifying work of the Spirit and the sealing work of the Spirit as acceptable to him. Tell him that he who will name the name of the Lord must depart from iniquity. This is what it means to accept Christ and the Spirit of Christ upon gospel terms, which is called faith (John 1:12).

[4.] *Appropriation.* He must be coming unto Christ, stretching out his soul to lay hold on him, opening his heart to embrace him, flying upon the wing of desire to draw near him. Thus, faith is expressed by "drawing near" (Heb. 10:22). Though he cannot draw near with full assurance of faith, yet he can with full sail of affection. Faith is expressed by "embracing the promise" (Heb. 11:18). Though he cannot embrace the promise as having received it for his present portion, yet he embraces it as seen from afar. Faith is expressed by laying hold (Heb. 6:18). Though he cannot lay hold of Christ as his treasure and possession, yet he lays hold onto the hope set before him. Faith is expressed by "coming to Christ" (John 6:35) saying, "I am unworthy to come near him, yet he is worthy to be obeyed, and he commands me to come. Though I am not sure he will receive me, yet there is no way but ruin if I do not come. He invites me, and who knows but he may receive me? I have no one else to come to. The world I have renounced, and to come to it is to run upon the sword of an enemy. My lusts I have forsaken and to return to them is to run back into ruin. There is none but Christ, none but Christ to whom my soul can come for refuge. And lo, he calls me; behold, I come unto you, for you are the Lord."

[5.] *Resolution.* Having come to Christ, he resolves to continue there. If he dies, he will die at Jesus' feet. If he perishes, he will perish with Christ in his arms. If justice seizes on him, it shall cause him to fly to the horns of the altar. Nothing shall frighten him from his hold. "Come death, come hell," he says, "I will not let thee go." Nay, the more he is afraid, the faster he clings. "When I am afraid, I will put my trust in you" (Ps. 56:3). "Though he slay me" (as he may justly say), "I will trust in him" (Job 13:15). Those that find him dead shall find his heart and hands fastened upon Christ. As nothing shall frighten him, so nothing shall persuade him to leave his hold. He answers as Ruth did to Naomi, "Wherever you go, I will go" (Ruth 1:16).

[6.] *Expectation.* Being thus resolved to cleave to Christ, he expects something from him. Though his hopes are weak, his hold is strong. There is a hope before him though he does not apprehend what he lays hold of. Although he cannot come to the throne of grace with that full assurance of hope which the apostle mentions, yet he has a sweet breeze of probability, enough to keep him in motion and to hold his head above water, and this may support him in the meantime. "The expectation of the poor shall not perish forever" (Ps. 9:18). Though it may stick upon the flats and dash now and then against the rock, yet it shall not perish. Or though it may seem to perish for a time, yet it shall not perish forever.

(4.) The special encouragements which this faith may have in reference to the success of prayer:

[1.] This relying upon God engages him to answer, and the Lord will not fail his engagements. If one relies upon a great person for a favor and has encouragement from him so to do, it will not stand with his credit and honor to disappoint him; much less will the Lord fail those whom he has encouraged to depend on him. He is tender of his honor. If such a soul comes to him and tells him, "You have invited me to fly to you for refuge. I have no one else to defend me. I have renounced all other dependencies. If you fail me, I perish." He that flies to the Lord for refuge shall find in due time strong consolation. Christ will not deliver those up to justice who fly to him for sanctuary.

[2] Christ highly commends this faith of dependence. He seems to admire it and be extraordinarily taken with it. "Speak the word only, and my servant shall be healed" (Mat. 8:8). Here is expressed a faith of dependence. If there is any assurance, it is but a half assurance, that which respected the power of Christ, not his willingness. So it is in Matthew 15 with the woman of Canaan—Christ drove her off from all assurance; that which she asked was not proper for her. "It is not good to cast the children's bread to dogs." Nor was he sent for this purpose. He leaves her no ground for assurance, yet by this faith of dependence she clings to him, pleads with him, urges him so far till he yields, till she prevails, and she prevails as far as she will. See here the power of this faith put forth in prayer; it can prevail with Christ for the obtaining of all we desire.

[3.] The obedience of one who has a faith of dependence in seeking God is in some respect more excellent than the faith of those who have assurance. For a child that has his father's smile and love to be affectionate and obsequious is no great matter, but for one whom his father does not own, who knows not that he shall have any share in the inheritance, to be obedient and affectionate, this is excellent and rarely ingenuous. So for one that is assured of the love of God, walking in the light of his countenance and knowing that heaven is his portion, it is not much for him to be fervent in seeking God and waiting on him; but for him who sees nothing but frowns in the face of God and has no assurance of any reward for his attendance on him, to be much in prayer, eager in following him, diligent in waiting on him, this is obedience of a rare ingenuous temper and cannot but be highly acceptable in the sight of God. For one to say as the martyr, "Though I know not that Christ loves me, yet I will die and be burned for him," will not the

Lord value such an affection? Will he not reward it? Will he not make sweet returns to such prayers?

[4.] He that has this faith of dependence has an interest in all the privileges that attend assurance though not in his own apprehension. This faith justifies the person, and since the person is justified, the prayer is accepted. This gives an interest in the covenant, and he that is in the covenant has a right to all the promises. This proves interest in Christ, and he that has that has interest in Christ's intercession, his Father's love, and his Spirit's assistance. What more is required to make prayer successful? If prayer is accepted, it will be answered though he apprehends it not.

Second, there is a false confidence to be found in the prayers of unregenerate men. We see too many who are confident as to their state of salvation. They may be as confident that their duties shall be accepted as that their prayers shall be heard when they pray for salvation. As nothing is more dangerous, so nothing is more common than presumption. They are so high and strong that one of the most difficult works of gospel ministers is to demolish and level these confidences. This is one of Satan's strongholds wherein he secures natural men against the assaults of the law and the gospel, which are the means to bring them to surrender and yield themselves to Christ upon gospel terms. Such confidence we see in the Pharisee (Luke 18). The prophet declares against it in the degenerate and profane Israelites (Amos 3:9-11). Here the question is how the confidence of faith may be known and distinguished from presumptuous confidence; how a true believer may discern that his confidence in approaching God is not the presumption of hypocrites; and how presumptuous sinners may be convinced that their carnal boldness is not the confidence of faith, so the prayers of faith may be distinguished from the prayers of presumption and carnal confidence.

Ans. The confidence of faith in prayer differs from this presumptuous confidence in its rise, grounds, attendants, and effects.

(1.) In its *rise.* The carnal man arrives at this confidence, but he does not know how. If we should say to it, as the master of the feast to him who lacked the wedding garment, "How did you enter here?" he can give no satisfying answer. He can give no rational account how he came by it. He has had it ever since he can remember, ever since he was accustomed to pray. He attained it with ease; it cost him nothing. It sprang up in him suddenly, as a mushroom, without his care or industry, whereas the confidence of faith is not in an ordinary way so easily attained. True believers remember how their carnal confidence was cast down by the spirit of bondage and their spiritual confidence was raised with difficulty by degrees. It was a work of time and labor, like the casting down of mountains and the filling up of valleys. After the convictions of sin and wrath, their own vileness and unworthiness made a valley in their spirits, undermined their mountain of presumption which stood so fast, and laid them low and vile in their own apprehensions. It was a work of difficulty to raise their souls to this confidence. They found fearfulness and confidence struggle in their souls as Jacob and Esau (Gen. 25:22) or Perez and Zarah (Gen. 38). With doubt and fearfulness putting out the hand before this confidence could break forth, the soul was in the meantime, as it were, in travail.

(2.) In the *grounds.* Presumption has either no ground at all or else it is raised upon nothing but sand; in some, it springs from their natural temper. They can be bold and confident with men, and they will be so with God. He may complain of them, "You thought I was altogether like you" (Ps. 50:21). Their apprehensions of God differ little from those they have of men, and so they make bold with him as they do with their familiars. They sometimes ground it upon their prayers, especially if they are long and often in this duty. They think they oblige God and conclude something is due them from God upon this account, and accordingly they expect it. Hence, it is that when the returns do not come as they expect, they are ready to expostulate with God as though he did them wrong, like those in Isa. 58:2-3. Sometimes, they raise it upon the same foundation with the Pharisee (Luke 18). They are not so bad as some and they do more good than others, so they are confident that they shall fare well at God's hands. But the confidence of faith is to be found in those who are most bashful and modest as to their natural constitutions but now are renewed and fortified by the power of grace. Christ and the promise is the ground of this confidence. They rest not in their prayers nor any part of their own righteousness. They know that all their shreds put together will make no more than a menstrual cloth, a garment both ragged and loathsomely spotted. This is an occasion of shame and blushing; they can have no confidence to be seen in such a woeful habit. They count all their prayers, abstinences from sin, and actual righteousness but loss, look on them all as lost, and have no confidence to be found anywhere, in anything, but in Christ (Phil. 3). But what the grounds of it are, I have given a large account before.

(3.) In the *attendants.*

[1.] Confidence of faith is accompanied with reverence, which is a filial and holy fear of God. The apostle, who so often exhorts the Hebrew believers to draw near with boldness, confidence, and full assurance of faith, makes reverence attendant with faith. Let us hold fast this confidence, and thereby we shall be enabled to serve God with reverence. Hope (often put for faith and confidence) is joined with fear (Ps. 147:11). "In the multitude of your mercies, there is confidence" (Ps. 5:7). A believer is sensible of his own vileness and apprehensive of the majesty and holiness of God. He has low thoughts of himself and high thoughts of God. These thoughts impress upon the soul an awe-filled respect of God and an ingenuous dread lest any action or word should pass him in this duty not beseeming such a majesty. He fears anything that might be in the least bit offensive or dishonorable to God. He is like a child who is most afraid to offend his father when he is close to him. The presumptuous have good thoughts of themselves but low thoughts of God. The Pharisee was an emblem of such. In his prayer, he is more praising himself than praising God. Or if upon any occasion their thoughts of God are raised, yet they are so slight and powerless as to leave little or no impression upon the heart. The higher they rise in these speculations, the weaker is their influence, like high stars that give little light. Their apprehensions leave no awe or dread of God upon their hearts. Or if there are any impressions of fear, yet it is a fear of suffering from him rather than of displeasing or dishonoring him. As slaves that would not dread the displeasure or disparagement of their master, they are afraid of stripes and blows.

[2.] There must be a resignation of his will and wisdom to the will and wisdom of God if his prayers are to be accepted. He will be content with God's will, time, measure, and way as to the answer of his prayers and the circumstances thereof. But presumptuous confidence must have what he desires or nothing, when he expects it or not at all, in the way and degree he wants, or else it is not worth the having. It is a proud stiffness of spirit. His will must be the rule to measure his answers; his wisdom must judge what is best; these must not veil nor lower to the will and wisdom of God. He is like a sturdy beggar that must have what he asks or else you must look for ill language from him. If the Lord will not punctually gratify his desires, he has hard thoughts of him, murmuring and repining against him like the Israelites in the wilderness. A tender plant will bow and bend to the will and pleasure of God, but counterfeit confidence is like a sturdy oak or a dry stick that will break rather than bend.

(4.) In the *effects*. Confidence begets fervency. We see by experience where there are hopes of attaining something that they will quicken up to eagerness in pursuing. A duo confidence of receiving will make a believer vehement and fervent in asking. The apostle makes a prayer of faith be a fervent prayer. James 5:15, which is a prayer of faith, is described to be a fervent prayer (ver. 16). Elijah is given as an instance of one praying in faith. His prayer is expressed by this character of fervency (verse 17), literally, "he prayed in his prayer"—as a form of speech, it is usual with the Hebrews to express vehemence through repetition; he prayed in his prayer, meaning, he prayed vehemently. Those who are truly confident in God *pray* their prayers, others do but *say* their prayers.

If a man desires a thing above himself and has hope that he may reach it, he will stretch himself to do it. This hope, this confidence of attaining what we desire of God, will make our prayers be a stretching of our souls to God. According to the import of that expression in James, an extended prayer was made, a prayer wherein the soul was extended and stretched out to God.

That prayer which springs from this confidence is a soul-labor, the travail of the soul. The heart is in labor while it is in prayer. But the prayer of the presumption is but lip-labor, a labor of the outward man, a bodily exercise. The heart and affections are cold, dead, without lively motion. Or if there is any heat, life, and fervency in them, it is but at some times and for some things. There may be some eagerness at sometimes, as when they are under some strong or sharp affliction. "In their affliction, they will seek me early" (Hosea 5:15). Then they seek diligently, but at other times, carelessly.

Or they may be eager for some things, for temporal blessings, for outward deliverance. They may howl upon their beds for corn and wine, but not for holiness, not for power against endeared lusts. They pray for temporal things like Augustine did before his conversion, as if they were afraid to be heard. Or they may be affectionate in some parts of prayer. There may be some heat and importunity in prayer when their necessities of outward things are pressing (Isa. 26:16). They poured out a prayer. Their hearts, as though they were dissolved by the ardency of desires for deliverance, ran out in their petitions. Oh, but was there any melting, confessing, or bewailing of sin?! Was there any heat and affectionateness in their praises of God?! No. When such are to offer a sacrifice of praise, there is no fire on the altar, no heat nor ardor of affection, no fire from heaven, at least nothing but strange fire, such as their own interests and concernments kindle.

(The original sermon appears to be unfinished.)

FINIS

Made in the USA
Columbia, SC
15 March 2021

34262020R00046